MW00879239

Learning to Believe the Unbelievable:

Living Life as a Miracle Leader

Stephen McGhee

AuthorHouse™
1663 Liberty Drive, Suite 200
Bloomington, IN 47403
www.authorhouse.com
Phone: 1-800-839-8640

First published by AuthorHouse 2/14/2008

ISBN: 978-1-4343-6643-6 (e)
ISBN: 978-1-4343-6641-2 (sc)

Library of Congress Control Number: 2008900784

Printed in the United States of America
Bloomington, Indiana

This book is printed on acid-free paper.

TABLE OF CONTENTS

ACKNOWLEDGMENTS

Acknowledgment pages are a very interesting part of any book. I have often wondered how an author could discern, and ultimately decide, who to acknowledge for the genesis and the production of such a Herculean project.

After completing this manuscript, I began that process myself. I sat down and wrote for quite a ***long*** time. When all was said and done, my acknowledgment page was more than an entire page in length. I had lists of people from my past and my present that I wanted to thank.Did I remember everyone?

As I reviewed that list of amazing souls, a simple thought occurred to me. The truth is that I have absolute gratitude and appreciation for ***every single person*** that I have ever met or has been a part of my life, no matter how brief or sustained the relationship. Every book, movie, TV show, coach, client, teacher, student, friend, relative and even every conversation I ever had has contributed to the person I am today. These people have helped me upon my journey and have all become part of my story. They have been part of the tapestry of my life which allowed me to establish and deepen my understanding of what I know to be Miracle Leadership.I began to see that those that have challenged me the most have also been a great contribution to my life and my learning. Rather than placing a list of names in this section, I decided to handle this part differently.

So in essence, I want to acknowledge my life and ***all*** those that have played any part in it. I am grateful for all of you, for all of it...for that is what has really led me to this place of my tremendous inspiration. Most certainly I would acknowledge the role of Spirit in my life. My greatest expression comes from God.

Peace.

Introduction

Learning to Believe the Unbelievable:

Living Life as a Miracle Leader

How many times have we accomplished something that at one time we thought was impossible? Our lives and our past are full of remarkable results achieved in the face of disbelief. This book is dedicated to the people who are inspired by that...people who love the idea of transforming the ordinary into the extraordinary. Through this book, you will learn to believe the unbelievable while learning to live your life as a Miracle Leader.

What would your life be like if you lived every day as a miracle? How would you feel when you woke up in the morning? How would you approach your work and family? What would you do differently in your life?

Have you ever felt stuck in some areas of your life? Have you ever become complacent and comfortable in your approach to living fully? If this describes you in any way, know that others feel the same. Even though you are not alone, it is now possible for you--- through the use of this book--- to find a better way.

Finding a better way will be exhilarating, scary and fun all in the same breath. But if you trust this process and breathe deeply into the possibility of becoming a miracle leader, you will realize that you are as divine as anyone else. If not you, then who?

Too Long Stuck In Your Rut?

Let's say, like most people, you have been stuck in a rut. You probably had no idea what to do about it. But now---through this personal journey of discovery---you will learn how to become "un-stuck" and live more freely.

Perhaps you can relate to the following mental scenario:

My eyes are barely open, and the first thoughts for the day come flooding into my mind.

I am still tired. I lost my temper with my assistant again, and I feel resentful for all of the work I have to do. Why do I get handed the toughest projects? Why can't my boss see how hard I work? Crap, I'm gaining weight again. My doctor says I shouldn't eat sugar, but I want that Danish in the fridge. Oh God. Is tonight the night I'm supposed to have dinner with the neighbors? Why does Mary make plans when she knows I'm so busy? The neighbor's dog is such a pest. If I could just win the lottery, my life would be better. I thought my life would be different than it is. I feel stuck. I wish I could sleep all day.

Can you relate to this scenario? Have you ever woken up in the morning and been bombarded with your own stressful thoughts? Have you ever felt exhausted before you even stepped foot out of your bed?

Let me introduce you to: Rut-free Living

For the past 17 years, I have devoted my life to learning about people, and much of that time I have spent learning about myself. In my experience, I have found that we have more in common with each other than most of us realize. Perhaps it is part of the human condition, but most of us judge far too many things throughout the day as good/bad or as right/

wrong. We create anxious expectations about how things "should" be, and when our experiences don't match up to these expectations then we are disappointed. This is a no-win mental roller coaster ride, and fortunately there is a way off the ride.

Interestingly, I have found dramatic similarities between some of the most powerful business people in the world and individuals who have very few business skills: Both people want to make a difference in the world, but they just don't know where to begin.

In my quest to better comprehend the human endeavor, I made a decision that if I was to understand what makes human beings live with purpose, I would need to experience my own life fully with no regret. There have been occasions where I have felt forced to look closer at my life than I could have imagined. These introspective occurrences have deepened me as a leader and have given greater meaning to my life. Through this book, I will share with you the personal experiences that have led me to where I am today.

Who's the Real Boss?

After receiving my Bachelor's Degree in Finance and a Master's Degree in Spiritual Psychology, I developed an awareness of leadership so profound that I could see connections between otherwise obscure situations. After years of applying what I had learned to coaching other leaders, I realized that leaders were not necessarily people who hold the greatest authority in a given position. True leaders are people who have enthusiasm for their own lives and an inner drive for something much greater than themselves. From their convictions, amazing results occur in all parts of their lives. They exemplify leadership by creating daily miracles.

How's Your Quality Of Life?

As I continued my study through becoming a leadership consultant and living my own life of leadership, I began to see that the quality of life that miracle leaders experience is different from most. Unlike the masses of people who work in jobs they dislike or who crave recognition for their unappreciated contributions, miracle leaders have an intention and focus that is devoted to something much bigger than they are. (Some devote themselves to business, communication skills, and/or charity events. Others dedicate themselves to improving awareness of global climate change, and/or to raising a family guided by loving support. In all cases there is a higher good---a bigger purpose at play in their lives.)

While each case varies, these leaders share a certain key attribute---a love of life! Once I saw this common thread between these successful individuals, a new definition of leadership emerged for me.

Soon it became clear to me that true leadership was an organic process that had more to do with an individual's willingness to learn than the position he or she holds at work. Leadership is a collaborative effort leading to a common result.

These amazing individuals that I now call miracle leaders seem to "make things happen," turn projects around, and develop deep and meaningful relationships. Being led by their inner focus on a higher purpose, these leaders create miracles on a daily basis.

But what exactly is a miracle? According to Webster's Dictionary, a miracle can be any of the following three definitions: **1**) an extraordinary event manifesting divine intervention in human affairs; **2**) an extremely outstanding or unusual event, thing, or accomplishment.

Accepting these definitions, is it really possible to *create* a miracle? In my experience, the answer is a very definite "Yes."

Once I had a greater understanding of the true process of leadership, I realized that these methods could be replicated through the study of the common attributes of leaders. Each one of us has the power to create miraculous results. All of us can be "Miracle Leaders."

What is really possible with "Miracle Leadership?" ***Anything is possible*** with miracle leadership. If anything is possible through leadership, then ***miracles*** can be attained through this process.All we have to know at the beginning is how congruent the concepts of miracles and leadership are. We must know up front if leaders are living their lives as though they were miracles.

Enjoying the Marrow of Life

Miracle leaders view situations differently than others do. They view life as an organic, moving process---a viewpoint that leaves them more open to life and its many changes. They enjoy their personal and professional lives, and this love of living manifests miraculous results.

For example, in the influential movie *Dead Poets' Society*, Robin Williams plays a miracle leader. He is a boys' prep school English teacher who encourages his students to "suck the marrow out of life." What would your life look like if you sucked the marrow out of it? What would be different when you awoke in the morning?

The following suggests the mindset of an individual who is applying the elements of miracle leadership. Contrast this to the mindset I illustrated earlier:

I slept fully. I'm learning to be more patient with my assistant, and I'm grateful for his support especially because I have such a full plate at work. I'm thankful for being trusted on this project. Once this project is done, I'm going to go on a vacation to reward my hard work. Today I'm going to the gym at 6 pm. My doctor says I shouldn't eat sugar, so I'm going to have that protein shake he recommended. I want to make sure I return Mike's book back to him at dinner tonight. I'm glad that Mary handles all of the social events in our lives. Jake, the neighbor's dog, loves to follow me around. I have such a great life. I feel like I won the lottery. I love how my life is turning out. I'm looking forward to starting my day.

They Reap What They Sow

While miracle leaders may still experience an "inner dialogue," they are *inspired* by their own head chatter. They are present in each moment, and they view life as an extraordinary gift for learning. With their willingness to look deeply and honestly at their lives, these leaders create their own methods for exploring what I will call their "Inner Landscape." Because they are willing to work the soil, plant the seeds, pull the weeds, and fertilize their intentions, these leaders "grow" miracles which are not always easy to produce, and they savor the fruit that their actions bear.

And Now a Gift for You

If you are interested in living an outstanding life, this book is dedicated to you. It is a book dedicated to the creation of miracles in your life, and to your recognizing that you *are* a miracle. *The Miracle Leader* is also devoted to the awareness that bringing out the very best in you will positively influence those around you. This book offers you a way to take an honest look at your life. It gives you an inspired perspective on the possibilities for change. And if you read this book from cover to cover and honestly answer all of the questions, I promise you that your life will take on the miraculous quality we've been talking about.

I want you to feel comfortable with this book. Know that this was written for you to experience just as though you and I were sitting together chatting over your favorite cup o' joe. While you may not agree at first with every idea that I have written, I trust that you will take the concepts that work for you and leave the rest behind. Then, when you read this book a second time, new levels of opportunity will open up to you. This book is meant to be used like a durable tool.

When enough people live from a more inspired perspective, the world takes on a more miraculous quality. You yourself can be the person that gets the process started. I invite you to discover with me the miracles waiting for you in your life.

Intention, Intention

My intention is that this book brings you results. It is based on my successful consulting work with leaders all over the world. So it's based on what works. If you follow the simple exercises within, I will make three promises:

1. This book will transform your old concepts of what a leader is into the possibility of becoming a "Miracle Leader."

2. You will create a "miraculous result" through the practicality and the application of these principles.

3. You will enjoy sharing this book with other communities and organizations craving new results.

Consider how exciting and invigorating your life would be if you created miracles on a daily basis. Imagine how your relationships at home and at work would transform. You have the power to make this your reality. So let's begin.

Chapter One

My Own Life-Changing Miracle

In the spring of 1990, I experienced a miracle that changed my life forever. I spent 11 nights in the intensive care unit of a hospital in Denver, Colorado. I walked into the hospital on an early evening to have a swollen bicep checked. I had hurt myself several days before while lifting weights in the local gym. I remember thinking that I had torn a muscle in my bicep, and yet some part of me knew that it was much more serious than that.

The nurse took me to radiology where they began to run a series of tests including an x-ray. One procedure showed the path of blood in the veins and arteries of the body. My path was blocked and it showed an occlusion of six inches in length along my left bicep. An occlusion is suspected to be a blood-clot, which can be deadly if the clot breaks off and travels to vital organs in the body. The medical professionals moved quickly with expert precision. While the doctors and nurses prepared for a treatment which would hopefully dissolve the clot, I called my brother Sammy and asked if he would come to the hospital. Though we weren't particularly close at that time, I was so grateful to know he was coming to be with me.

While waiting for my brother, I began to think about my life. A million questions ran through my mind as I watched the doctors and nurses work busily over me. How did this happen? What had I done to deserve this? Is this how quickly life can change? Had I already fulfilled my purpose in life?

Because the doctors were concerned that the clot would break off and move into my lungs, they injected a drug into my veins to dissolve it. The liquid drug filled my body. It moved quickly through my system, and within seconds, I had a metallic taste in my mouth. I felt the warmth of my brother's hand in mine.

I was terrified.

I felt my body temperature drop. I was getting cold and I started to shiver. My body began to shake uncontrollably. The nurse's face grew ashen. People came from nowhere. My heart slowed down. My body had rejected the drug. Right then and there my body stopped functioning altogether. I went cold, and I went away.

I was an ocean of intelligent information. I was a drop of the ocean and I was the entire ocean. I was nothing and everything all at once. I was you, and you were me. It was peaceful perfection. There are no other words to describe it.

The nurses injected me with another drug that counter-acted the blood thinner, and slowly my body warmed up as the blood began to flow with ease through my veins. While I don't remember much about those moments that followed, as I opened my eyes again I do remember the profound love that I felt for my brother. It was as though I looked at him with new eyes. My relationship with Sammy has never been the same since, and to this day I share a deep and powerful love for him. I was given a second chance to live my life with new meaning.

My Life Up To That Point

By all practical standards, my life prior to this experience was good. I was upwardly mobile in the banking firm for which I worked. I had owned several properties at an early age. I was having fun with friends, and I was seeing new places. The outside appearances of my life were "good," and yet something was missing. I felt a void. I was lonely even when others were around me. I was so busy trying to prove something to myself that I truly didn't live life. While some would say I looked happy on the outside, I was deceiving myself on the inside. I did not really like my job or the people with whom I worked. I wanted to experience freedom, and yet I had no idea what real freedom meant until that memorable evening in 1990.

Seventeen years later, I am still trying to fully understand this remarkable experience. For years, people have asked me if I died. I do not know for sure what happened because where I went did not seem like death. It seemed like life. I know my body stopped. I know that I had an experience that changed my life. I know that my experience gave me information about my life that I previously did not have. My experience in that particular moment was one of extreme peace. There was a feeling of knowing blissful perfection in all places and at all times. I was lifted to a place of understanding that to this day I cannot completely explain. Clearly, and with much gratitude during those moments of surrender, I knew that my life would continue. I had been forever changed.

The Certainty That Miracles Do Happen

As time went on, I began to understand that miracles do take place in people's lives. My whole life has become an inquiry into how to convert that enlightenment into an expression of leadership. Because I have learned that if I can live life as an everyday miracle, so can you.

From an early age, I can remember being fascinated by 'adult' conversations. I was impressed by the formality and confidence with which people spoke. Years later, as I became a communication specialist I continued to be intrigued by these same conversations. But now, I question their genuineness.

Is it possible to have a genuine conversation? Absolutely. Not only that, the more you have, the better you lead...yourself and others. There have been times in my life when I was more genuine or "transparent" than at other times. My conversations with family, friends, clients and business associates all offered chances for me to observe this. And once you can observe it, you have power to increase your authenticity in all things.

Rather than pointing outwardly to my business associates, for example, I have learned to look inwardly to better understand my levels of communication with others. I have found that my relationships with others are a direct reflection of my relationship with myself. In other words, when I am withholding my truest thoughts and when I am not as open and honest as I can be, my relationships both with myself and with others suffer.

I have learned that by being more "real" with the people around me, there is a magical quality and depth that occurs in those relationships. I am not talking about drama, or wounds from the past. I am talking about bringing "real" presence into my conversations.

The miracle here is that anyone can do this. For example, when you meet by chance a friend in your office building and he asks how you are doing, do you genuinely reply how you are feeling at that very moment? Or, do you simply say "Fine, thanks, and you?" Imagine what your relationship would be like if you *really* answered your friend's question. I realize this idea is counter-intuitive to what many of us hold as a subconscious belief: it's safer to be inauthentic. But like many ideas in this book, you will be stretched to some new ways of approaching every day situations.

Do You Have Stagnant Beliefs?

Before reading further in this book, I challenge you to ask yourself the following questions: How is your current way of doing things working? If the status quo is working for you, and you are experiencing truly high levels of communication in your relationships, then perhaps your approach is the best one. But if you are not, then you have nothing to lose and everything to gain by engaging in a new approach. And this new approach may require you to be more open than in the past.

Living as a "Miracle Leader" begins by accessing that new level of openness. Your past beliefs (such as, "It's safer to be inauthentic") will be challenged as you begin to open yourself up to the people in your life. You might feel nervous, or afraid, or you might even feel that some people will mock you for being so open, honest, and vulnerable. It will take practice. But I promise you this: it will create relationships that are built on trust and support.

I want to develop that level of trust with you today. As the writer of this book, I feel I have a responsibility to you to clearly and adequately convey the elements of "Miracle Leadership." Taken individually, these concepts are not "new," and yet when these ideas are woven together they create surprising new power in your life.

How Are Miracle Leaders Different?

Miracle leaders are open to miraculous results. Miracle leaders see that everything that occurs can be used to support the growth and learning of an individual, team, and/or community. They are individuals who find solutions to all situations, and they vigilantly create positive outcomes. These are men and women who put themselves wholeheartedly into the game of life and participate with every ounce of their "being." Rather than looking to the past as a reference point for future possibility, they follow their intuition and search for "unreasonable" results. When others say that something cannot be done, a miracle leader will still seek to find a way. These people live life with clarity, and they will not compromise their integrity.

Miracle leaders can be counted on to do what they promise they will do. They are clear on what they want, and they are willing to do whatever it takes to make things happen. Miracle leaders do not wait for others to speak up or to lead; instead, they carry the level of confidence of true leaders. Through inspired leadership, these people are consistently in action.

Miracle leaders exude strength, love, respect, and compassion for all humanity. They have a magical way of listening and exploring the deeper meaning in what is being communicated to them.

As a miracle leader you will embody the following elements:

1. Being open to miracles
2. Using "Letting go" as a miracle in itself
3. Trusting miracles through full participation
4. Knowing the miracle of your discomfort
5. Living the miracle of integrity
6. Being the miracle of your word
7. Listening as a miracle leader
8. Expecting miracles from clarity
9. Knowing you are a miracle
10. Implementing miracles
11. Living in the spirit of miracle leadership
12. Know that loving is the ultimate miracle

After reading through this list, you may feel that you already embody many of these qualities. Regardless of where you begin, this book will demonstrate each of the twelve elements to becoming a miracle leader.

My goal for you is that you create your own relationship with this book. I want you to *feel* this book, as if some part of your Soul has come alive. In order to accomplish this, you need to allow yourself to see yourself in new and inspiring ways.

Get Off Your "Little s"

To begin the exciting process of seeing yourself in a new way, you must give up your little "s." That's right: you will keep your Self, but not your self. And you know what the big Self is: it's the part of you who knows what is best for you.

The "little s" *self* feels threatened by new ideas, and is therefore comfortable with being "just ok." The "little s" already thinks it knows the answers because it is ego-based. It tends to "run the show" and will do anything to be right, as it does not want to look or feel insecure.

The "big S" Self, on the other hand, is the part of you that contains your greatness. It is the core of your being. It eagerly seeks new and exciting ways of expanding horizons through more powerful and courageous means. Open to new ideas, the "big S" Self is more interested in integrity than showmanship, and it creates exciting possibilities for the highest good of all those involved.

Once you master taking the perspective of your big Self, you will be open to exploring miracles. So it's time to go deep into that Self with Self-questioning: How would our approach to life change, and what would it mean if you began to believe that you really are a miracle? By learning to make this shift in perception, you will begin to create results with ease in all areas of your life: business, relationships, health, finances, and spirituality. Your life will no longer be something mundane that just "happens" to you. Instead, your life will become a work of art and a gift to behold. It means you will have the experience of living your life as a miracle leader.

After 17 years of studying leadership and working with leaders all over the world, I have come to understand what elements in situations make an influential difference in a person's life. From this perspective, I have observed miraculous events. I have seen good things occur in people's lives when they thought there were no more options. When a person is open to new experiences, anything can happen—even miracles.

The first step toward being a miracle leader is to develop your willingness to inquire about life. Soon you will love all the questions that life brings to you in all its many forms. By blending your enthusiasm with an open sense of "not knowing," you will participate as a leader who both creates and awaits the many miracles life has to offer. With this new approach to your daily life, you will begin to notice what happens when you participate fully in every moment of your life. You will gain new experiences: the colors are brighter, the tastes are bolder, the sounds are sweeter, and the tangible results are greater.

> *"Miracles, in the sense of phenomena we cannot explain, surround us on every hand: life itself is the miracle of miracles."*
>
> **George Bernard Shaw**

Chapter Two

LETTING GO CREATES MIRACLES

Since my near-death experience, I have been blessed with grace beyond compare. I have realized there is nothing to lose or to be afraid of, and the only way to live my life is by being true to my Self.

You, too, can be grounded in your purpose, living moment to moment while being completely focused on a vision for your life.

Begin by answering this question now: What do you want for your life? And if it feels hard to decide, try this: What have been your greatest experiences? When was the last time you let go of resentment and blame, and grabbed hold of total acceptance and trust?

Life is too valuable for you to remain complacent.

There is a metaphor I use in my leadership seminars that always creates deep breakthroughs for people. Try this now for yourself: Imagine for a moment that you are a trapeze artist. See your Self standing on a platform hundreds of feet up in the air. Imagine you are looking down and feeling the excitement and the fear of being up so high. You look in front of you and see the platform on the other side. Does this distant platform represent a goal in your life?

You have "a platform" where you would like to go, and more often than not it brings up fear. For as long as you can remember you have wanted to achieve this goal, yet some part of you has held your Self back. You begin to rationalize why you "should" or "shouldn't" do this. But how will you ever truly know if something is right or wrong for you? Look inside and you will find the right answer. Only you can do this for your Self. Reach out and grab the trapeze bar, and jump from your safe platform to your goal platform. You feel the emotion and exhilaration as you fly through the air. You must grab the other trapeze bar to get to the new platform. Now is the time to transition from one bar to the next. I ask you, what must you do to catch the new bar? What must you do to embrace a new level of miracle leadership? You must let go. If you let go, you will reach the new platform and enjoy a new life experience. If you are not willing to let go, you will hang on to the old bar and eventually lose momentum.

While being open to miracles is the first step to miracle leadership, you must also be willing to "let go" of your past so that you may embrace new possibilities. By learning to create a space from which you can produce miracles, you are able to generate positive outcomes. These positive outcomes can occur in starting a new business, involving yourself in community projects, or creating closer family relationships. There is no limit to where it will show up. Because *letting go* gives you access to freedom, inspiration, and commitment.

There is Hidden Power in "I Don't Know"

May I share a secret with you? If you don't know something, it does not make you weak. It makes you real.

By admitting that you don't know something, you create compassion that allows you to identify more authentically with people. Whereas pretending to know something you really don't know pulls you out of integrity and makes you weak. One of the most important elements of living life as a miracle leader is your ability to say "I don't know."

If you can accept the idea that you don't know something, then suddenly you access an open and unlimited field of inquiry where you can find out the answers. You don't have to try to remember what it is you are pretending. You can open up completely. You soon become a master of engaging others around you who can help you find the necessary solutions to life and business. This skill is critical for you in becoming a great listener and communicator. It makes you a vessel for learning. You will feel the paradoxical power of humility by having the ability to "put yourself out there" by asking questions that engage higher levels of cooperation and collaboration.

Just Let Go!

Leaders don't need to have a near-death experience to access this level of consciousness. To create new ways of living, leaders must first be willing to let go of past constraints and ideas that do not serve them. This will go against the norm, because most people are holding on to ideas that keep them "blocked." I don't want you to continue being one of those blocked people. I want you to make all green lights and fly down the highway of life. For this to occur, you will have to "let go." You'll have to throw out the areas of weakness that no longer serve you.

Have you ever noticed that sometimes you learn more from painful growth than easeful comfort? Recently, I was considering how I have grown more from my areas of discomfort than from my areas of comfort. And because I want to live a transformative life, I have realized that often the best action to take is the action that makes me least comfortable. So I've begun to look for opportunities to just let go and embrace a new behavior. I have learned that "feeling life" means getting out on its edges, being willing to make mistakes, and working hard for the things that are most important to me.

Over the years, hundreds of people have told me that they feel as if they are just hanging on. Day in, day out. Just hanging on. Can you relate to them? What would your experience be if you just let go of your old beliefs in exchange for a new experience? Would you feel nervous? Would you feel excited? What's the difference? Why wait any longer? Why not start now?

If you become true to your Self and your path of life leadership, you will begin to notice great changes and miracles in your life. Your attachments will fall away, and you will make room for new experiences.

> *"The invariable mark of wisdom is to see the miraculous in the common."*
>
> **Ralph Waldo Emerson**

Chapter Three

THE MIRACLE OF DISCOMFORT

I want to encourage you to play your edge, and step outside of your box. Your limitations are nothing but an illusion. Limitation seems real to you because that is all you may know. I too have lived in the comfort of my old limitations.

Several years ago, my good friend Terry Tillman taught me a simple concept about life. While on an extended *Wilderness Experience*, Terry took a stick and drew a simple circle in the sand. "The circle," he said, "represents everything that up until today you knew to be true, and it represents your level of comfort." He continued, "Everything outside of the circle represents everything that you feel is outside of your level of comfort, things that challenge your existing truth." He paused and looked each one of us in the eye. I looked at the circle and felt queasy. He said, "Let me ask you a question. Where do you think the greatest amount of learning is for you? Is it inside or outside the circle?" With his steely blue eyes, Terry looked at me and asked, "Guess where we are going to be spending most of our time in the next 10 days?" We all laughed and said, "Outside of the circle."

With a rush of energy, I felt alive in a way that I had not felt moments before. My face, my voice, and most importantly my relationship with my Self began to change in that very moment. While I was nervous, I was more excited than ever to be alive. I was becoming a miracle leader.

During those ten days a whole new world opened up to me. Though I woke up nervous everyday, I felt myself changing from the inside out. I

I accomplished things that before I did not think were possible. Because of that trip, I have greater levels of freedom. I now look for the miracles of each day, and I "live" to live. We all have the same zest for life and it is up to each one of us to lead ourselves forward into our own expansion and expression.

Time to Take the Stage

William Shakespeare was exemplary in producing miracles. According to Shakespeare, "All the world's a stage, and all the men and women merely players" (*As You Like It*).

Your own life is a drama that you have created. So if you are the lead character in this play called life, are you starring in a comedy, tragedy, or romance? There is nobody more responsible in how you experience your life than you. You are the producer, director, and star of your own play.

Now is the time for you to move from victim to a more starring role. One of the very first steps to living a miraculous life is getting you to see that sometimes your life's skit is *boring*. Why would that be? Why would you ever have a skit or story line that does not support you in fulfilling an exciting dream?

Can I Get My Money Back?

Imagine going to a Friday night talent show with friends where each person in the audience gets up and does a skit about their life. My guess is that you would leave before intermission. People's lives are boring.

But yours doesn't have to be. So take a hard look: Are you stuck in the repetitive skit of your life? Do you live the same story over and over again, somehow thinking that this time you will see different results?

At one point in your life your current story line was probably interesting to you, so interesting that you may have become stuck—stuck in a rut reliving the same (lack of) drama. The most loving thing I can say is: Stop boring yourself. You are putting yourself to sleep. It's time to wake up and write a new scene in your life.

There have been times in my own life where I was stuck in my own script. Life was no longer colorful, and my daily experiences had become monotonous. Once I realized that I was stuck, I took action and rewrote my script. I reevaluated my life and the part I played in it, and I opened myself to new possibilities of transformation. I was not special. This reevaluation is open to anyone. I teach it to people every day.

What Kind Of Script Do You Want?

How do you want to live your life? Do you want a life of monotony where everything is bleak and gray and your relationships are complacent, or do you want a life full of color, freedom, and adventure where your relationships are deep and meaningful? You have one life to live; how do you want to create your miraculous life? You can transform your life at any moment, and only you have the power to do so.

Sound unreasonable? Good!

You may be stuck in being "reasonable" about your life. If so, you are adept at rationalizing positions on things that continue to support the direction of your existing script. This kind of rationalization can keep you locked into old stories. You've become so accustomed to this robotic, repetitious behavior that you don't even know when you are doing it. Waking up to this fact can be exhilarating.

Stop Being So Reasonable

My brother Douglas and I recently led a trip of people down to Chile to experience ten days of white water adventure on the Futa River. This was an extraordinary opportunity for people to see an amazing part of the world and to be with 15 other adventurous individuals. In planning the trip, I encountered some interesting rationalizations, and they went something like this:

Stephen: *I am planning a trip down to Chile to raft one of the world's greatest rivers. I know how much you enjoy this sort of trip. You've worked so hard and it would probably do you a lot of good to take a break. Would you like to join us?*

Reasonable Person: *I would love to go. I have always wanted to do something like this.*

Stephen: *Great! Can I get you signed up and committed?*

Reasonable Person: *(looking like a deer caught in the head lights) Hmm… When is it?*

Stephen: *It's from the 12th-23rd of February.*

Reasonable Person: *Oh, I could never leave work for that long. Judith tried to get off of work for two weeks last winter and she got turned down. Besides, how much is it?*

Stephen: *If this is something that you really want to do, it couldn't hurt to ask your boss for time off. We got a special rate through the rafting company, and the trip is $3750.00 all-inclusive.*

Reasonable Person: *(deer in headlights look again) Man, I don't know what I was thinking but I don't have that kind of money to blow on myself. I have kids, a mortgage to pay, there's just no way around it.*

Stephen: *I can understand that. If you are willing, I would be more than happy to spend some time coming up with different ways for you to make that money. It will take some effort on your part, but I know we can do it.*

Reasonable Person: *Listen, I really appreciate all of your help, but it's just not a good time for me right now. Maybe I'll go next year.*

How many times have you been on one or the other end of a conversation like this? One of my primary purposes in life is to help you see life as a miracle. And if you are consciously playing the leading role, you can live life any way you choose. You can come from that place of *unreasonableness* where you produce great results. Rationalizations are as tricky as Homer's six-headed monster, Scylla. As soon as you have fought off one, another appears.

Unreasonable Expectations

In this famous (and useful) quote, 19th century Irish dramatist George Bernard Shaw writes,

"The reasonable man adapts himself to the world; the unreasonable one persists in trying to adapt the world to him self. Therefore, all progress depends on the unreasonable man."

Being an unreasonable person in this context does not mean to act outside of one's integrity; instead, it simply means stepping out of your mental box, letting go of fearful expectations and *participating fully in life.* You'll no longer read from the same script of your past, and you'll look inside your larger, truer Self for new ways of living.

Now let me share a true example of a conversation with someone who is not afraid to be "unreasonable":

Stephen: *I am planning a trip down to Chile to raft one of the world's greatest rivers. You have told me in the past that you love this sort of thing, and so I thought of you. Would you like to join us?*

Unreasonable Person: *Sounds great. I love that part of the world. I deserve something fun after all of the work I have been doing this fall. I need to talk to my wife and kids before I start making plans. I'll let you know tomorrow.*

Next Day

Unreasonable Person: *I talked to my wife and she was excited for me. Though we have to figure out the work and school schedules, I know we can find a way. Also, I can't put a deposit down until two weeks after the due date. This is not a great time financially, but I know I can make this happen. I owe this trip to my Self.*

Stephen: *I know you will be there. I am putting you as a solid "Yes," and I will extend your deposit date out two weeks. We are going to have the time of our lives.*

Miracle Leader Expansion Process

When faced with a new experience, my process for expansion is as follows:

1. An opportunity is presented to me where I may expand into doing something new or different.
2. I evaluate whether or not I am interested in participating in the experience, and I question if it is for the highest good of all those concerned.
3. Initially I feel a sense of fear, self doubt, and insecurity as to whether I will succeed or fail.
4. I realize that fear is just my comfort zone being challenged.
5. I immediately reference the times in my life where I have grown from recognizing this feeling.
6. I take action in the direction of the experience, event or opportunity.

What can you do today that will begin a process of expansion?

If Not You, Then Who?

You must realize by now that this exciting concept of deliberately moving outside of your comfort zone can apply to most everything you will do in your life. For example, you may have had a misunderstanding with your cousin that has gone on for years and has caused unnecessary tension at holidays and family functions. You don't like her, and she seemingly doesn't like you. The impact of this behavior is that your relationship with her father, or your uncle, is less intimate and this divisive behavior cascades into the relationship with your family members. You see the impact on your family yet, you don't really do anything about it; instead, you stay comfortable being uncomfortable.

After several conversations with family members, you realize that you have a part in the situation and that it is your responsibility to end the discomfort not only for your sake but also for the sake of your family. You decide to call your cousin and you have a forthcoming conversation with her over lunch. At this point, there is nothing to lose and everything to gain. With this conversation, you create a possibility for moving the relationship forward. She is surprised. She agrees. You are a miracle leader within your family.

In the past, you might have questioned why you should be the one to "make things right." You should be the one simply because you can be the one. Even if you don't do it for the other person or your family members, you owe it to your Self to live from a place of enlightened integrity. You will begin to see that miracles can occur through your leadership from being unreasonable.

Put Your Right Foot Out

A few years ago, I was leading a business seminar for a non-profit organization that had been stuck in a rut for several years. Though 15 years ago the organization carried a profound message to over a million people and made a great difference on our planet, their business model had not changed with the times. There had been attrition, shrinking exposure, and scarcity. Their organization no longer felt powerful.

Because their levels of comfort were so fully integrated into the organizational structure, they strongly resisted any suggestions for change. They had closed off all possibility of discussing new ways of being "unreasonable," and they sank deeper into their boxes of comfort. To this day, the organization struggles with the same issues as they continue to read and act out the same script over and over again. What are they missing? The one thing they don't have: a miracle leader.

So How Will You Know?

You will notice you are stuck in the comfort zone when:

1. There is a feeling of constriction in the stomach and throat areas.
2. People are not having honest conversations.
3. The same ideas are constantly brought up, yet no action takes place.

You will notice the comfort zone is expanding when:

1. There is a feeling of alignment in all areas of the body.
2. People are open, honest, and genuinely listen to one another's ideas.
3. Execution on action steps is consistent and sustained.

Time to Throw Out the Old Script

I believe that most of us have reasonable and comfortable scripts about our lives. We want to live amazing lives and have amazing relationships filled with joy, yet most of us have become complacent over time. Life has so much more to offer than mere comfort.

> *"Miracles are not contrary to nature, but only contrary to what we know about nature."*
>
> **Saint Augustine**

Chapter Four

THE POWER OF INTEGRITY

Once on a New York to Munich plane flight, I sat next to a man named Cliff who was busy studying Italian. He had been studying Italian for five years, and he challenged him Self to learn a few new words every single day. Cliff told me that the "consistency of things is more important than the speed of things," and he spends 30 minutes a day learning Italian "rain, sleet or snow."

My new friend Cliff is 86 years old and holds the demeanor of a seasoned miracle leader. He spoke to me with lightness in his heart and intensity for his convictions. I could feel something very special about Cliff: he lives his life with integrity.

As we reached 39,000 feet, Cliff shared with me some of his life stories. He had owned several businesses and had "failed" in a number of them. Yet, Cliff's perception of his life was that of success. He spoke of his failures with the same enthusiasm as his successes. His life was colorful and his experiences were meaningful. He never once spoke poorly of the people in his life, and he regarded his former wife as highly as his current bride.

Cliff loved his life. I was inspired by his presence, and I was appreciative of the gift that he had given me. I can only imagine the positive impact that Cliff has had on people throughout his life. Following my conversation with Cliff, I had a better understanding of what it means to live with integrity. Living life from one's core truth is living with integrity. In other words, living with integrity means you are living from <u>your</u> truth.

What Is, Is, No Matter What I Want It To Be

Recently, I went through an extraordinary inward shift. By most standards, my life was ideal, and yet my "inner leader" was screaming at the top of his lungs. I had become complacent, and my life was monotonous. I wasn't challenging my Self, and I began to settle for "just ok." I realized that I was no longer living in my integrity. I was afraid to change my life, but I knew that I had to do something. By taking the time to listen to my Self, I was taking the first steps in creating miracles in my life.

Sitting in the comfort of my home, I began to take an honest look at my life. I asked my Self what life would be like if I were completely free of my self-imposed limitations. What would I do, and what would my life look like? What results would a new life offer me? After contemplating these questions, I began to look at areas in my life that caused me discomfort. To what was I attached? How complacent had I become? How had my life been affected by my complacency? How could I best live my life, while simultaneously creating and achieving results? Finally, how could I take my relationship with Spirit to the next level?

After several days of contemplating these questions, I began to take action. To the dismay of my friends, I leased out my home the following week and began a homeless world-wide journey of self-exploration. The journey I began is what I now call "Living Life as a Miracle Leader," and the results have been profound.

Is Being A Miracle Leader Really A Risk?

By listening to my heart, and connecting to my integrity, phenomenal results have occurred. I have:

- Experienced the single most lucrative time in my business in over 12 years of leading organizational change.
- Interviewed 17 incredible leaders from diverse backgrounds.

- Written and completed this book.
- Traveled to four foreign countries that I have always wanted to visit.
- Experienced the most intimate conversations with clients, friends and random meetings with amazing people.
- Seen preserved wilderness I previously didn't know existed.
- Savored blissful moments on long highways.
- Observed nature's beauty (such as watching Orca Whales feed on mouthfuls of salmon in the Puget Sound).
- Had adventures beyond compare (Class V white water rafting in Chile, etc.)
- Disengaged from everything in my life that no longer serves my journey of integrity.
- Faced my fears and living my life to its fullest.

I am experiencing miracles, both professionally and personally, on a daily basis. I have become a miracle leader.

I Did It My Way—You Do It Yours

I am in no way inviting you to live your life as I have done; rather, I want you to explore your own deepest integrity. Take a few moments to ask your Self what kind of ideal life you envision. Who would you be if you listened to your inner leader, and then put into action what you heard? You are not exempt from this calling. Each one of us has the chance to live the life of our dreams. Get quiet, look inside, listen honestly, and you will know your deepest purpose. Your integrity will not deceive you.

A Good Definition of Integrity

We have all heard the word "integrity," and perhaps you have used it a few times when giving a company lecture. But do you really know what it means? More importantly, have you *experienced* integrity?

I recently asked a senior leader of a major organization what it meant for him to be in his integrity. He replied, "I don't really know when I am in my integrity, but I can assure you that I know when I am *out* of my integrity." Like most people, this leader has a hard time defining it yet he understands the power and essence of integrity when it is missing.

In Webster's, Integrity Is Only A Word...

While Webster's Dictionary defines *integrity* to be "an adherence to moral and ethical principles; soundness of moral character; honesty," these terms don't even begin to suggest the positive ways your integrity can influence others when you know how to access it and feel it.

How can you access this power for yourself? And how can you apply it to your daily life?

1. First, you must be completely honest with your Self.
2. Then, you must devote your Self to a path of miracle leadership.

While this two-step process may seem very simple, it is not always easy to live a life of integrity. However, the good news is that it does not need to be done perfectly. If your intention is to live your life from a place of integrity—and you begin to make movement in that direction—you will begin to see unbelievable results.

Integrity Is an Experience

Integrity may have existed for you in the past as an abstract concept—some kind of ethical guideline that made you nervous whenever it was brought up.

We're going to change all of that. From this moment on, integrity for you will be more of an experience, an *active* experience. By living in your integrity on a consistent basis, you will learn the freedom that comes with it. Your life will no longer be lackluster, and instead you will awake each day to the possibilities of new creation. You will feel good about your professional and personal decisions, and you will begin to feel like a new person. You will find that this "newness" has been with you all along. You just didn't know how to find it. But now, with a deeper understanding of your life's possibilities through your integrity, you will create experiences that you once believed unbelievable and unreasonable. You will create miracles.

Dare to Look

Beware! Don't fool yourself by not taking an honest look at your own integrity. You may have become so adept at seeing when others are "off course" in their integrity that you have lost focus of your own. It is the rare individual who has the humility, self-esteem, and foresight to put the focus on her first instead of others. No one wants to be under the "proverbial microscope" because of what might be found.

What's At Risk?

Remember that all egos are fragile. While you are in a process of conversion, when your ego feels the scrutiny, it will want to clam up. Put away the padlocks and the fenced gates. Trust your Self and know that true adjustments come out of areas of discomfort. Your only serious risk is to stay the same.

The Power Is Within You

This process is not for everyone. If everyone were ready for this, everyone would be reading this book. This is for you. It is no mistake that you are reading this book. So trust that this is the exact right time in your life for you to experience heightened levels of freedom and grace through integral living. Notice the phrase I used: integral living. That's the expanded power of integrity when it's experienced: integration of all your powers. In other words, you are hitting cleanly on all cylinders. So be fearless in what you discover about your Self. No matter how much you dislike what you may find, you have the power and the authority to alter your life's experience.

Two Lists, Two Worlds

From the two lists below, consider which of the following characteristics or situations you tend to experience more often and reflect upon the ones which resonate with you the most at this moment.

Column A

1. Lack of humor
2. Low physical energy
3. Same communication problems with different people
4. Conflicts avoided
5. High levels of stress
6. Agreements constantly re-negotiated
7. People avoid talking to you
8. Life's challenges overwhelm you
9. Resentment for people or situations
10. Low levels of productivity

Column B

1. Feelings of free expression
2. High levels of enthusiasm/adventure seeking
3. Interesting dialogue with others
4. Challenges met head on
5. Feeling of peace
6. True to your word
7. People love to spend time with you
8. Light about Life
9. Joy from people (and dogs!)
10. Results magically created

The temptation will be to label one list "bad" and one list "good." I suggest you consider Column A, *Off Course* and Column B, *On Course*. In other words, the characteristics from Column A indicate that a person is no longer living in their integrity, while the characteristics from Column B indicate that a person is living from a place that aligns with their integrity. These columns can act as a self-referential guide for evaluating whether or not you are aligned and integral in all parts of your life.

Know Where You Are Going So You Know When You Have Arrived

For years I have been teaching leadership sessions in organizations and have started most of these seminars with a simple yet difficult concept:

Leadership is an inner journey that produces outer results.

Until you are clear ***inside of yourself*** about who you are and what is important to you, you will continue to struggle in your daily outer life on projects at work and relationships at home.

While you may believe that taking an inner journey is narcissistic if not a waste of time, I have learned that ignoring this inward process creates a life of misery and self-deception. Though you may claim to be "content" living in complacency, you must inevitably face your fears; no one is exempt from experiencing an inner process.

What Will I Get?

Life will begin to hold new meaning. You will no longer fear the unknown, and you will experience increased levels of freedom. You will view life through the eyes of a miracle leader.

A miracle leader must begin with inner transformation. You cannot deny your Self the growth that comes from experiences, regardless of whether or not you see their value at that moment. Life is about learning, and in order for you to lead others you must first be willing to lead your Self.

What Does It Mean To Be Alive?

In preparing to write this book, I set forth on a journey to find who I considered to be miracle leaders. I began by interviewing ordinary people who were living extraordinary lives. I conducted interviews spontaneously, and I "fell in love" with many amazing people. I soon realized how many truly inspiring individuals produce miracles daily and continue to contribute to the good of our global community.

I met people from "every walk of life." From businessmen and women to artists to store clerks to educators, I loved them all. They are tall and short, muscular and thin, shy and boisterous, and they all have one thing in common: their eyes sparkle with life. They embrace life fully—both the bitter and the sweet—and they understand that each experience in life gives them an opportunity to practice living in their integrity. Simply put, they love life.

With each interview, I walked away feeling recharged and lifted by their powerful, infectious energy. Based in courage and love, these people were living life as miracle leaders.

> *"Miracles happen every day. Change your perception of what a miracle is and you'll see them all around you."*
>
> **Jon Bon Jovi**

Chapter Five

Being the Miracle of Your Word

A few years ago, a dear friend of mine was preparing herself to die. Because she knew she was going to die from a terminal form of cancer, she was able to say her goodbyes to friends and family.

During my visit to the hospital, I asked her a simple question: "What is the one thing you would have done differently in your life?"

She smiled, looked me straight in my eyes and said, "I would have said 'No' a lot more than I did. I said 'Yes' to many things that were not really that important to me because I wanted certain people to like me. Yet, those people are not here in my final hours. I would have spent more time with the people who I love the most."

She smiled one last time at me. I later learned that she died that afternoon. Her words continue to inspire me.

Imagine a world where people are brave enough to say "no" more often, so that "yes" can mean more, too. Imagine people simply doing what they say they are going to do. What possibilities could manifest if your team or family did everything they said they would do? Most likely, there would be an efficiency to life that you have yet to experience. What would your world look like if you always kept your word?

Your life would run more smoothly because you could depend on things being accomplished on time.

I learned from my dear friend's last words that keeping your word does not always mean saying "Yes."

I have also learned that there are essentially two ways you can keep your word if you have agreed to do something:

1. Do what you said you would do.
2. Renegotiate what you said you would do.

How can renegotiation be defined? By beginning with what is *not* renegotiation. Renegotiation does not mean sending an email that says you cannot make your agreed meeting time. While your willingness to let it be known that you cannot make your original time may be appreciated, there is no renegotiation in it. Instead, you are simply breaking an agreement.

A true renegotiation implies that both parties in the original agreement have agreed to a new change and have rescheduled the agreement together. And if the other party is not willing to renegotiate, you must be willing to complete the agreed action.

Check The Box

There are essentially three kinds of people in life:

1. People you can count on.
2. People you are not sure you can count on.
3. People you know you cannot count on.

While someone may fall under category two or three, this does not mean that this person can *never* be counted upon. Nor does it mean that they can't be loved for who they are.

For example, I have a person in my life on whom I simply cannot count. While I love this person, I can't trust whether or not she will actually do what she says she will do. I have learned that sometimes she follows through on her promises and other times she does not.

Regardless of how much I care for her, if she is consistently breaking her word then our relationship is impacted. If you have experienced a similar relationship like this in your life, you have two choices:

1. Disengage from the relationship.
2. Lower your expectations to avoid disappointment.

Rather than "pointing the finger" at others, you will be much more responsible if you consider how *you* actively can make positive changes in your *own* life. When determining your own levels of accountability, ask yourself the following questions:

1. In what areas could I be more accountable?
2. What can I do to be true to my word?
3. Can people trust that I am going to do what I say I am going to do?

Sticks and Stones May Break My Bones

Recently, I worked with a corporate team that was deeply steeped in dysfunction. Although they barely communicated with one another, the few words they did share were spiteful. Too often they made promises they didn't keep, and they responded negatively to one another. They spent so much energy berating one another that they wasted tremendous solution-based resources.

After we worked through some of the initial hurt and betrayal, the team dynamic began to shift. I asked the team to go around the room and share what they appreciated about one other.

Some people responded with excitement, while others rolled their eyes. One gentleman crossed his arms and asked, "Why do we have to do this touchy-feely crap? I mean, what does this have to do with business?"

I smiled, paused, and said, "Good point. Let's keep on working 65 hours a week with people who can barely talk to one another and who are pretending to be effective in business."

He smirked. I held the space and repeated the question. Before I knew it, it was after 7:30 pm even though the training session was scheduled to end at 6:00 pm. I sat in awe as angry relationships melded into relationships of respect and appreciation. I watched miracle after miracle occur as people began to develop functional relationships.

The Gift of Your Word

Some people consider gifts to be luxurious items such as cars, or vacations. You can also give someone a nice sweater, buy them a great meal, or share your dessert with them. But if you want to give someone a gift that will truly last a lifetime, *give someone your word.* Your word is the most precious gift you have to give.

A few years ago, I began playing an experiment with my Self. I pretended that everything I said had a monetary value. Every time I spoke, I "spent" a little money. As a professional speaker this was a real test for me. I noticed that while I was using a lot of words to speak, I was actually saying very little. My word-bank "charges" were going up. On the other hand, as I listened, I received money in my communication bank account. I soon realized that this was more than an exercise in humility.

At the end of several days, I would have very little in my communication bank account. Interestingly, I noticed that the more I spoke, the more promises I made. The more promises I made, the less likely I was able to keep my agreements with people. I wasn't as connected with people when I was doing a majority of the talking, and only after I began listening did I feel connected. When I was connected, I was making agreements that I knew I could keep. I no longer needed to talk all the time to feel better about myself. Instead, I was enjoying living in my integrity by keeping my word.

Do I Have To?

Have there been times when you said that you would do something in a moment of inspiration or excitement, and you were later challenged to do what you said you would do? For example, you may run into an old acquaintance at the grocery store. After a few minutes of catching up on each other's lives, you both promise to get together some time soon. After you exchange business cards, the card goes in your wallet and falls into a black hole. Did you agree to do something like call someone when deep-down inside you know you won't do it? It's silly, really. You're both too busy, and you both know it likely won't occur. So why do you make promises over and over again? Are you just being polite? Instead, say "I am so grateful I ran into you and I'm glad you are doing so well. Take care, and perhaps I will bump into you some other time." It's clean, honest, and full of integrity. You have nothing to do, and you are keeping your word.

Everything that you say and do impacts both your life and the lives of others. One way to recognize this is by observing how other people's choices impact *your* life. How do you handle a situation when someone does not follow through on their promise? Do you have trouble believing them when they give you their word again?

I Am My Purpose

In terms of creating magic and trust in your relationships, it is imperative that you are a person on whom others can count. Of course, this does not mean that you need to be a "Yes" person, especially if you do not believe in or have time for a particular commitment.

The starting point for living my word is a clear sense of purpose. When I am unclear about my own inner purpose, I am much more likely to make agreements that do not inspire me or support my growth. Then, the all-too-familiar cycle of complacency begins.

The cure for that is purposeful participation in life. Because once you trust your full participation, you will keep your word and your life will take on a new and peaceful meaning. You will experience greater freedom, and you will have clear intentions when making decisions. You will have more time to devote to your highest priorities.

The Power of Accountability

As a leadership coach, I have agreements with my coaching clients that I will meet with them face to face. One time I had a scheduled appointment with one of my coaching clients on a day that I was also offered a lucrative opportunity in a different city. I sent my client a request to do the appointment by phone. She sent back a very honest and thoughtful reply stating that for her it would be a compromise to agree to the change. She felt that the dynamic of being face to face in our coaching conversations had more impact, and at that time in her life that is what she needed. While I wanted to take the opportunity out of town, I was moved and inspired by her commitment to her Self and to the coaching work we were doing together. I immediately sent back a message agreeing to keep our existing agreement. The result of the coaching on that day was profound, and once again I was fortified by the power of this work in creating and deepening relationships.

Being the Change

During one phase of my life, I broke many agreements with people. After being faced with the wreckage of my decisions, I learned how much more efficient and enjoyable life was when I decided to always be accountable. Now, I say what I will do, and I do what I say.

Ask your Self the following questions:

1. How well do you keep your agreements?
2. What are you willing to do to be more accountable to your Self as well as the people in your life?

Who I Am is My Word

While you may identify yourself as being a human, a woman, or an architect, what we all have in common beneath all that is our word. I am my word and you are your word. Your word is powerful, and carries weight just as much with your colleagues as with your family.

When you speak, your words can either carry the deepest essence of your heart and soul, or they can reflect your surface temper and your irritability. Your words can be full of anger, blame, betrayal, or they can be filled with love, respect, and trust. So be mindful of what you say to your team, your family, and your loved ones. What you communicate to other people can never be taken back. Ultimately, once it comes out of your mouth it may be forgiven but it is likely not forgotten. Yes, you can pray for forgiveness, and you can say you are sorry. Certainly we all make mistakes. But if the words that come rolling off of your tongue are full of negative emotion, catch them as soon as you can. Apologize, look inside, and explain why you are so angry. Speak from a place of honesty, and speak with compassion.

Then let newer, truer more loving words reflect who you are and watch those words create miracles in your life.

Words Will Never Hurt Me?

Keep your word with yourself, too! You are the most important person with whom you keep your word. How do you talk to yourself? Do you constantly beat yourself up by telling yourself that you are too slow, too fat, and too stupid? Or, do you support your Self by being honest and compassionate?

For example, you can either berate yourself by saying "I'm a loser because I have the lowest sales this month" or, you can support yourself by saying: "When I am focused on my key accounts, I increase my sales." Your words to your Self will make all the difference in how you feel on a daily basis. Remember we saw that letting go is a miracle. So consider letting go of your harsh words.

> *"If future generations are to remember us more with gratitude than sorrow, we must achieve more than just the miracles of technology. We must also leave them a glimpse of the world as it was created, not just as it looked when we got through with it."*
>
> **Lyndon B. Johnson**

Chapter Six

LISTENING AS A MIRACLE

About 15 years ago, I met a woman named Katie with Downs Syndrome. I was sitting alone in a coffee shop, and Katie sat down uninvited at my table and began speaking about her life.

I was immediately frustrated that she had invaded my space. But because she spoke so slowly, I had to force myself to become more present to the conversation so that I could understand her.

She told me about how she tore tickets at the movie theater for a living and had to take the bus two hours before work to make sure she wouldn't be late. She told me that it took her several hours to get ready in the morning because she had to dress, eat breakfast, and take care of her dog.

At that time in my life, it felt odd to me that someone was sharing such personal things with a total stranger. I felt uncomfortable, and quite frankly I wanted to tell her how busy I was. After all, I had emails to write, stocks to check, phone calls to make. But in that exact moment of my impatience something amazing occurred. I stopped listening to my head chatter and started listening to *her*—her being, her Self. The noise in the background suddenly went away just as the noise in my head began to fade. Time slowed down, and I began to notice a foggy sort of veil around Katie. My eyes began to well up. I was present.

As she spoke and shared about her life, I felt as though she was peeking into the light of my soul. She was open, vulnerable, and willing to be present, and I was listening to her essence. I was sitting in a coffee shop with a complete stranger, and the most important thing to me was the next word from her mouth. All that mattered was this moment in time. After a while, Katie needed to leave for her job. She stood up, looked into my eyes again and said, "You understand me, don't you? I mean, you really get me, don't you?" She wrapped her arms around me, said good-bye, and I watched her walk away.

Since that morning, I am not the same person. Katie taught me how to listen. I have seen Katie a few times at the theater, and every time she smiles at me I am reminded of our lifetime bond that occurred through listening on that day.

I have been blessed with similar experiences hundreds of times since that morning fifteen years ago. Katie was the first person to whom I had ever really listened. She was living her life as an open and honest miracle, and that morning I received a great gift.

Let Me Listen To Who You Are

Once I had the experience with Katie, I decided I wanted more of that "realness" in my life. I notice now that when I am truly present to a conversation, I experience a deep sense of transformation. Rather than merely listening for content, I have learned to listen for the speaker's essence. In other words, I may silently ask myself, "What is this person really saying? What is she really feeling? What are her fears? What is she passionate about?"

I have learned that people really want to be heard. Too often we easily dismiss one another's words. Most of us want to share our ideas, feelings and thoughts, though it is a rare individual who can sit and be present to another human being. While it requires a lot of love and respect to truly listen to another person, it can be one of the most inspiring experiences on earth.

As I have practiced greater levels of listening, I have had one profound occurrence after another. I want to share a few of the comments that I have heard as a miracle leader:

I feel better, and nobody has ever listened to me like that.
I have never told anyone those things, and I just met you.
Are you spiritual or something? I feel different.
I have wanted to get clear on this forever…thank you.
I appreciate you so much.
Thank you for all of your help.
You're amazing.
My body feels physically better, and my head doesn't hurt anymore.
This is a miracle.

Making Time for Listening

If you are anything like me, you might be thinking any or all of the following thoughts: "I don't have that kind of time;" "Listening to someone go on and on about nothing is boring, and I don't care what they think;" "I have a company to run, I don't have time to listen to every Mark, Susan, and John;" and "I have heard it all before."

Do any of those thoughts sound familiar to you? The good news is that those fears are baseless. What I have found is that listening consistently over time actually *decreases* the amount of time you spend in conversations with people. In other words, you will develop relationships with people that take less maintenance and will function on a higher level of intimacy and trust. In being truly present in relationships, you will save time. Honestly.

I recently heard a speech by Peter Senge, the author of a book called *The Fifth Discipline*. In his studies on leadership he found surprising new evidence which showed that "listening" was the single most important element of leadership in the new millennium. During this portion of his presentation, it was the only time that day that over a thousand people really seemed to be listening. During those 10 minutes, I could hear people breathing. Time seemed to slow down, and there was a spiritual energy that replaced the frenetic energy I had felt just moments before. The room was left with amazing peace.

Energize Through Listening

I believe that when a large group of people are that intent on listening, there is a positive quality that fills the space. Think about it. When was the last time you were at your favorite sporting event and the home team was seconds away from winning? Do you remember the feeling? Something happens when we unite our listening—we get present. As a miracle leader, ask your Self the following question: What would occur if you could bring "listening" into alignment with your company's vision? What would that mean for your company and how would it produce results? Further, what would happen in your relationship with your spouse and/or children if you really listened to them?

Listening *can* be taught.

Entering the Powerful Spaces

Have you ever listened so intently to another human being that you actually could hear something between the spaces of their words? What did it feel like to be present fully to the conversation? Have you ever truly listened to the sound of your own breathing? What was your experience of being quiet inside of your Self? Did you connect with your inner Leader? What value is there in listening to the Leader inside of your Self that gives you direction for your own life?

Is Hearing The Same As Listening?

To me, listening is one of the most fascinating topics we could cover in this book.My experience is that many of us generally don't practice or think about becoming attuned to our own listening.

I was taught at a young age that listening meant that after hearing the content of what another person has said, I should literally be able to repeat back what I "heard" that person say. While this may be a great step in the direction of true listening, it does not give us the deepest understanding of another human being.

Listening occurs when you and/or the person have a sense of *complete and total understanding without judgment or blame about the content of the conversation.* This kind of listening requires an intimacy and connection with your Self and another human being that brings the relationship to higher levels of understanding. Like everything else in this book, I want you to understand a deeper context for what is possible in terms of listening.

The Plague Known as Head Chatter

There have been times in my life where I had so much "head chatter" it was nearly impossible to listen to another person during a conversation. I would nod my head up and down trying to appear to be a good listener, but then the head noise would begin: "I don't have time to listen to this right now. I have things to do. I wonder what time it is. I need to get going." I would sit with a pseudo-peaceful smile on my face only pretending to "listen" to the poor soul in front of me.

If you are like me, you can hear the language and content of a conversation, and yet there is no "presence" to your listening.

True listening requires you to be present in the moment. Therefore listening is not as easy as it may seem, especially if you have other pressing issues at hand. However the rewards for listening truly can be magical.

In order to listen to others, you must learn how to quiet that part of yourself that is incessantly trying to be right. Only then can you listen from a place of understanding and patience.

Can You Hear Me? Can I Hear Me?

It is because we have difficulty listening to our own higher Selves that we don't listen very well to other people. So the first step to being present with another human being is first to get present with your Self. This requires that you become quiet enough to hear your Self think.

Many people quiet their minds by doing yoga, meditating, going for long walks in nature, fly fishing, praying, journal writing, painting, etc. Recently, I recommended to one of my coaching clients that he take a small trip and simply be silent for a weekend. He kicked and screamed about it at first, and through the kicking and screaming he soon realized why I had made this recommendation. During his weekend of silence, he found a solution to a 10-year relationship problem that previously had "stumped" him. With this quiet "space," my client changed his own life forever.

I have found that you cannot really create miracles until a space is open where you can be present with your Self. You will know when you are quieting your mind once you feel a more peaceful feeling inside. You will be more relaxed in your thinking, you will get clarity on issues that have up until now been confusing and your true essence will sparkle through your eyes. The results of listening will emerge.

A Poem for You

Many years ago, I came across a beautiful poem on listening. Though the author is unknown, I have always wanted to express my gratitude to him/her for capturing the essence of listening within a poem. For years I have shared this poem with many different people, and today I would like to share it with you. Enjoy!

Please Listen

When I ask you to listen to me
and you start giving me advice,
you have not done what I asked.
When I ask you to listen to me
and you begin to tell me why
I shouldn't feel that way,
you are trampling on my feelings.
When I ask you to listen to me
and you feel you have to do something
to solve my problem,
you have failed me,
strange as that may seem.
Listen! All I ask is that you listen.
Don't talk or do---just hear me.
Advice is cheap; 20 cents will get
you both Dear Abby and Billy Graham
in the same newspaper.
And I can do for myself; I am not helpless.
Maybe discouraged and faltering,
but not helpless.
When you do something for me that I can
and need to do for myself,
you contribute to my fear and
inadequacy.
But when you accept as a simple fact
that I feel what I feel,
no matter how irrational,

then I can stop trying to convince
you and get about this business
of understanding what's behind
this irrational feeling.
And when that's clear, the answers are
obvious and I don't need advice.
Irrational feelings make sense when
we understand what's behind them.
Perhaps that's why prayer works, sometimes,
for some people---because God is mute,
and he doesn't give advice or try
to fix things.
God just listens and lets you work
it out for yourself.
So please listen, and just hear me.
And if you want to talk, wait a minute
for your turn---and I will listen to you.

Author Unknown

Take a few moments now to reflect on how well you listen by answering the following questions: What was powerful for you about this poem? In what areas of your life can you improve your listening? Now, do the following exercise and practice the art of listening through practical application.

Put your Self in a quiet, seated position where you won't be distracted.

Quietly ask your Self, "What can I do to be a better listener?"

If your mind begins to wander, get quiet, breathe, and ask the question again.

If there are specific actions you can take, please write those down now.

As a miracle leader, you will begin to see sustainable changes in your relationships at work and at home. You will experience greater levels of intimacy, and you will have a greater understanding of those around you. You will bring an engaging quality and essence to each of your conversations, and you will begin listening from your heart.

> *"Deep listening is miraculous for both listener and speaker. When someone receives us with open-hearted non-judging, intensely listening, our spirits expand."*
>
> **Sue Patton Thoele**

Chapter Seven

Miracles Come from Clarity

From growing up in a single-parent home, to reading my first "personal growth" book, to leading seminars on leadership, my life has developed into an incredible journey upward that continues to sustain momentum.

Like many people, I lived through the experience of my parents divorcing when I was very young. While I did not see my father for another 34 years, my mother worked hard to feed and rear four children. We always had just enough to get by. Yet through it all I learned that there were no limitations to who I could become in the world.

I believe that many people like me have been raised in "less than ideal" situations and have had painful experiences at a young age. That's just reality. But my question is this: Must we continue to blame our current lives on these past experiences? Must we limit ourselves by living in the past? Do we have to keep ourselves from experiencing true joy at present?

Why is it so common for people to do this? Is it part of the human condition or have we simply become comfortable in our own suffering?

Fortunately, there is a way out of this "comfort zone" of silent suffering. I've found the way in my own life and helped many others do the same. And if you follow the suggestions I'm about to make, it can now be *your* time to find the miracle of freedom from the past.

How to Peacefully Fight Your Limitations

In my early twenties, I remember staring at the cover of Dan Millman's book, *The Way of the Peaceful Warrior,* and becoming inspired by the claim that this was "a book that changes lives." While part of me thought that the idea that a book could create a whole life change was a ridiculous notion, my inner Self yearned to fill my void.

After reading that book, I found the claim on the cover was true. Because it began for me what was to become a journey of a lifetime. From that point on I began asking my Self tough questions about my daily interactions and choices. I began viewing every situation as a possibility for growth. Without knowing the words for it yet, I had begun thinking like a miracle leader.

I stopped blaming my single-parent upbringing for all of the "bad" things in my life. Instead, I viewed these experiences as greatly contributing to the man I am today. For example, because I didn't have two parents providing for me, I learned how to create opportunities for myself. At the age of 13, I learned responsibility as the neighborhood paper boy. I learned that I didn't have to rely on others for money, and from this experience I gained the confidence necessary for later becoming an entrepreneur.

While the process that I went through wasn't easy, I wouldn't trade my childhood for anything because I gained tremendous freedom from facing those challenges. I began to see all of the different ways I could apply my hard-won sense of self-responsibility. Not only did I create a successful leadership consulting practice (where I utilize these principles,) but I also realized something important about life. Life was much less complicated than most people make it. And life can be much more enjoyable than I originally had believed.

I now know for certain that my only limitation in life is myself.

The Power of Two Simple Questions

To continue the promise I felt in Millman's concept of the peaceful warrior, I began asking myself two very basic questions. Until I honestly could answer these two simple questions, I found that my life would remain "stuck" and uninteresting. But by bringing this simple inquiry forward and acting on it with integrity, I could develop a better understanding of what it means to live life as a miracle leader. By answering these questions, you too can achieve your life's greatest desires. And because these questions are practical, they can be used to support both new and current situations.

To grow as a miracle leader, you must first ask your Self the following question:

What do you want?

Because this question is simple and effective, it will bring forward areas where there is little or no clarity and it will simultaneously propel you in positive directions. For example, you may be struggling in your relationship with your brother. Because you have had a few failed attempts at creating a more meaningful relationship, you may want to reevaluate your approach by specifically asking your Self what type of relationship you want with your brother. Rather than typically answering that you want a meaningful relationship, you may answer that you would like to have: 1) Conversations with your brother that are rich and filled with truth and honesty and 2) Monthly adventures with him on fishing or skiing trips. By answering this simple question with complete honesty, your intention is set with clarity.

You may desire more meaning in your life and yet you are unsure of where to begin. The question "What do you want?" provides you with the necessary clarity to move forward in a simple and powerful way. Rather than focusing on what you don't want, this will place your mental energy and focus on the things you *do* want in your life. Once you know what they are, you can then evaluate the actions that will lead to your desired results.

And now to grow even further as a miracle leader, you must ask your Self the second question:

What are you willing to do?

This question will provide you with even more clarity. Now you can decide whether or not the value of what you want matches your willingness to take action.

For example, if you want to improve your relationship with your brother, there are multiple approaches you can take. One approach would be to sit down with him and let him know that you have realized that you are not as close as you once were. Let him know that you have missed him and that you would like to feel more connected with him. Some possibilities for this could be by having honest conversations as well as planning adventurous trips together. While you may or may not feel comfortable with this approach, you will determine how much it means to you to have an improved relationship by the action steps you are willing to take. This question offers you a simple method to evaluate the strength of your aspiration for improving your relationship.

These two questions will support you in many areas, no matter how big or little. As a professional coach, I continue to be amazed by the great impact these practical and supportive questions have on the lives of my clients. By asking your Self these two simple questions, your own life will also change dramatically.

From Suicidal Depression to a Miracle Life

One example of a man who used this process to attain his dreams is Michael Galli, a friend and former coaching client. Through his example,

Michael's story offers us a dramatic look at the experience of miraculous change. You will see that it all begins by asking your Self both what your deepest desires are and what you are willing to do to get them. While reading Michael's story, I recommend that you envision your own desires and keep in mind what you want for your life. And if you doubt the power of questions, notice that Michael says it was a *question* that saved his life.

Michael Galli's Story: September 2001 through 2006

Is it really possible to eat yourself to death? I hoped so. Killing me with food would be an easier way to die than driving my car into a stone wall. Yet, every night on my way home from work, I would contemplate how fast I would have to be going to make sure that I would die. Knowing my luck, I would end up paralyzed because I drive such a safe car.

After my wife left me on September 10th, 2001, I spiraled into a deeper and darker depression that only led to increased eating and the total loss of desire to do anything to help myself. I also was struggling in my relationships at work, and I only knew feelings of worthlessness.

During a yearly physical exam, my doctor asked me how I had been feeling. I responded that I was doing great at work and was making more money than I ever thought possible. She told me how happy she was for me and my good fortune shortly before congratulating me on being able to afford a really nice casket. She said that if I did not do something about my weight, I would be dead within a year. While most people would be startled by the news of a quickly approaching death, I was actually quite relieved. You see, I hated my life and I wanted out. I was almost 500 lbs, my wife had recently left me, and I hated my job. Why would anyone want to stick around and deal with this painful and worthless life?

Over time, I started taking painkillers to aid my aching joints. While they seemed to help the pain, I began toying with the idea of taking more pills to stop the pain for good. As I was questioning the purpose of my life, my thoughts were interrupted by the phone. My business consultant, Stephen McGhee, cheerfully said hello and asked how I was doing. At first I attempted to mimic his happy tone and pretended that I was feeling great. Of course, he didn't believe me for a second. Stephen began asking me question after question, which eventually led to the first "real" conversation I had had in quite a while. I told Stephen about my conversation with my doctor, and after some time on the phone Stephen engaged me in a conversation that saved my life.

After admitting that I did not really want to die, I realized how scared and lonely I truly felt. I was afraid that I did not have the inner strength to make the necessary changes to help myself. In a few words from Stephen, my life went from bleak to believable. This conversation created the necessary shift that saved my life. Stephen asked me what I was willing to do to live, and I replied with relief "Anything." He repeated back to me my words and asked me if he accurately understood me that I was "willing to do anything to live." I boldly exclaimed, "Yes!" At that moment, my life changed. Affirming to Stephen and myself that I wanted to live and was willing to do anything to save my own life, I felt a physical shift in my body. Everything clicked into place.

Since our conversation on that day in 2002, Stephen has reminded me often of my exclamation of being willing to do ANYTHING to save my life. This has led to many changes. Three months after our conversation, I quit my job, sold everything and moved to another state to begin my weight release process. I have since released over 320 lbs!

I now realize that I have the power to create the life that I want and deserve. I eat healthy and take care of myself. I am also self-employed and love what I do. I have surrounded myself with loving and supportive friends, and I can honestly say that I love my life. I feel so blessed to have created this second chance at life, and I am looking forward to my second trip to Argentina and Chile where I will raft in Class IV & V rapids, climb beautiful mountains, and swim in glacier-filled lakes. My life keeps getting better and better!

Being Open to the Miracle

By asking him what he wanted and what he was willing to do to get it, I helped Michael become open to the possibilities of miracle leadership. Inevitably, we all reach a choice point like Michael's. We all stand on the edge of change. Will we find the courage to move forward? Or will we let the chance pass us by and slip back into complacency?

Not all your choice points will be a matter of life or death like Michael's. You may even be succeeding in some area of your life while another part of your Self wants to take you to a higher level. Regardless of your specific objective, you can achieve it with the support of these simple but powerful questions.

Your Choice Points

If you do not find that your level of willingness fully supports what you want, you will need to revisit and adjust your specific objective. If you are not willing to do what it takes to achieve your desire—just *let it go for now* so that you can freely move on to the next area of focus.

> *"They say miracles are past."*
>
> **William Shakespeare**

Chapter Eight

Knowing I Am a Miracle

Many years ago, I was invited to teach miracle leadership to a team of executives at a major pharmaceutical company. This team was responsible for leading ground-breaking research on AIDS. The medication they researched was created to prolong the life of HIV positive patients. I looked forward to my session with them.

After speaking with the head team leader over dinner the night before our first session, I was intrigued by his remarkable accomplishments and I was a bit intimidated by his demeanor, particularly his need to control our conversation. He spoke in detail about his own background without talking at all about what I wanted to focus him on: his team's problems and concerns. In essence, the head "team leader" had skipped past the concept of "team" on his way to being a "one-man show." I was very interested to see how he would interact with his team and me the following day.

The next morning, the first thing I noticed was how quiet his team was rather than sharing information and being open to new ideas. As soon as there was a voice of *any* kind of dissent, the team leader quickly refuted the comment and regained authority. After an hour of witnessing this type of interaction, I decided that—as the facilitator for the session—it was important that I intercede.

I then challenged the team leader to take a moment and observe how his behavior as a leader might be constricting the team's success. The team leader responded angrily, pointing out to me that because he had four doctorate degrees he understood the problems better than anyone else on the team...and certainly better than I did...for I was just an outside leadership consultant.

He rhetorically asked if I was aware that he had a doctorate from MIT. In that moment, I knew that we were standing on the edge of a great shift.

I said, "You don't seem to understand that I don't care that you have a doctorate from MIT." Mouths dropped open as I asked him, "Who are you being *right now*? How are you showing up *today* as the leader of this team?"

I slowly glanced around at the relieved faces as the energy in the room became still. The team leader sat back in his chair and looked as though he may have just had the realization of a lifetime: Who am I being right now? I witnessed his heart open as his eyes filled with emotion. He had lived his whole life pretending to have all the answers. His faced changed in an instant, as though he had let go of his need to feign knowledge and control situations.

Later that night I sat with him at dinner. I noticed that he was more present in our conversation than he had been the night before. We spoke openly and honestly about his life. By always playing the role of expert, he had negatively impacted his wife and children, as well as his team members. He could see it.

He now realized that his role as a leader could mean allowing space for others to share their brilliance. He recognized that he had been micro-managing each member of his team rather than truly leading them.

To his benefit, he could now learn to see that leading people meant living from the leadership attributes I'd highlighted in our sessions. Leadership, he recognized, has very little to do with past knowledge and has everything to do with how he was participating currently with his knowledge.

I admired his courage to be honest and his willingness to assess his behavior in life. While the team dynamics did not change drastically overnight, that day paved a way for the team to share their leadership over time and eventually emerge as a team of 22 miracle leaders.

Am I *Really* A Leader?

Let's face it. Most of us don't see ourselves as leaders. We are more like the executive I just talked about. We try to manage based on hiding our own insecurities. So, when we hear the word "leader," we usually envision other political, religious, corporate, and sports leaders on top of hierarchical systems.

While this is the traditional perspective of the top-down approach, I want to explore with you a more progressive view that sets aside the typical configuration chart of an organization. Though it is possible that leadership occurs hierarchically, in the years I have been teaching I have met many managers and CEO's of organizations who have very little understanding or integration of leadership skills. Either these individuals rose to positions of authority from some skill set or, they had been with the organization much longer than other employees.

Many of us have been taught that leadership is based on a title. This is simply not true. Leadership is a demonstration of both a person's behavior and actions in a given situation.

Re-thinking Leadership

For years, I have conducted leadership-defining exercises in my seminars. I asked, "What are the top ten attributes of leadership from your perspective?" Often, people would sit and wonder about the right answer to the question. After a few moments, I would then ask them to think about the people in their lives they admired who had impacted them in a positive way.

At this point, people opened up. By remembering their experiences of leadership in action, they would let go of their past beliefs about leadership and instead they would view leadership more simply. They began to see leadership as how a person was "being" with them as opposed to what a person's title was.

Over a short time, the true, experiential attributes of leadership began to emerge with more clarity. From these attributes, the elements of living life as a miracle leader were formed.

The most common attributes that individuals listed as demonstrated by leaders were:

Column A	**Column B**
FROM **Leadership Attributes**	***TO Acting as a Miracle Leader***
1. Openness	1. Being Open to Miracles
2. Letting Go	2. Letting Go as a Miracle
3. Full Participation	3. Trusting Miracles through Full Participation
4. Outside of the Box	4. Knowing the Miracle of my Discomfort

5. Integrity	5. Living the Miracle of Integrity
6. Accountability	6. Being the Miracle of my Word
7. Listening	7. Listening as a Miracle Leader
8. Clarity	8. Expecting Miracles from Clarity
9. Self-confidence	9. Knowing I am a Miracle
10. Action	10. Implementing Miracles
11. Inspiring	11. Living in the Spirit of Miracle Leadership
12. Respectful of Others	12. Loving is the Miracle

Notice the congruency between the leadership attributes and the elements of a miracle leader. As I broadened my understanding of leadership, I began to see an amazing correlation between organizational leadership and my own exploration of miracle leadership. What I learned is that when all twelve of these elements are combined, then miraculous results occur. Furthermore, I noticed that these elements created "unbelievable" results when they were carried out into all parts of a person's life. Before I knew it, the compiled results gained in credibility. Not only that, when they were consciously applied people experienced miracles.

Who Are Miracle Leaders?

While further exploring these elements of leadership, I began asking various people if the individuals who play the role of "leaders" in their lives actually embody these leadership attributes in their personal and professional lives.

Overwhelmingly, the answer was no. People had a hard time thinking of people they would define as leaders based on the attribute list. No wonder we have lost faith in our leaders and ourselves. No wonder we have become cynical about making positive things happen in our lives and communities.

Not only are we no longer clear as to what we expect of our leaders, but many of us have subconsciously discounted our own ability to make a difference in the world.

But we have missed the point. Because the leader you are most looking for to emerge in your world is *you*.

Another Look

Take another moment to review the previously listed leadership attributes (Column A). From the list, what stands out most to you? Do you embody any of these qualities in your daily life? If so, how are they demonstrated?

Like many, you may look to others to lead you at work, at home, on your softball team, at the grocery store, or in a community meeting. But what do you do when someone is berating an elderly woman on the street corner or a colleague is "busting someone's chops" at a cocktail party? Being a miracle leader means recognizing that you are every bit as powerful and meaningful as the next person, and your beliefs are demonstrated through all your actions.

We have gone to sleep in this country. We have allowed ourselves to accept less than authentic leadership. Yet, we sit back and blame others. Or we blame the situation instead of seeing that leadership begins with you, me, your brother, your neighbor, your friend, as well as the CEO of your company.

How do we turn that around? Here's the first step: consciously set out to see something magical in the list of attributes that represents both you and others. In a perfectionist society, it is believed that you must embody absolutely every attribute all of the time. Not true. Just start somewhere. Find one attribute and build on it. Then move to another. You will evolve as you go.

Knowing You Are Divine

By maturing and evolving into a leader, you begin to realize that you are a divine human being. You have as much possibility inside of you as the next person, no more and no less. Whether or not you can embrace this idea right now, if you truly take the brakes off of your life and let your leadership light shine, your divinity will become apparent. You will understand, in a new way, the words of Teilhard de Chardin: "We are not human beings having a divine experience; we are divine beings having a human experience."

Because *you* are the great leader we were waiting for. Trust that you have the answers and qualities to make positive changes in our world. Stop waiting for the few select individuals we have voted into office or to whom we report at work. Take a stand for what *you* believe in, and let your voice be heard.

You'll begin to enjoy newfound opportunities to serve your Self as well as your community as a leader. If you are waiting to be given a new title or a position change, you are shortchanging yourself and others. You are hiding your greatness. As the creator of your own life's journey, you owe it to your Self to participate fully by no longer making excuses. Simply embrace the miracle leader within your Self as a new way of "being." You are a miracle leader. You always have been, and you always will be.

A New Way of Living

The key to this chapter is to gain the awareness that you are responsible for leading your own life. That in itself is the ultimate leadership challenge. As the leader of your own life, your decisions to be active or passive impact both your life as well as the lives of others. Once you realize your own power to practice miracle leadership, you will become aware of the differences you make. Miracle leadership will become a way of being that is expressed in all areas of your life.

Understandably, many people resist becoming a miracle leader. They are afraid to leave their comfort zones. They experience fear of the unknown. But know that you have a question that cries out to be answered: How do you want to live your life?

By exploring all of life's opportunities for growth, you will participate fully in your own life's journey. You will lose that feeling of *things always happening to you.* And you will be sharing the gift of life with those around you every day. Once you savor the taste of the freedom that comes with living a full life, you will never want to return to your old way of being.

While many people will be attracted to your energy, others may even feel threatened by your demonstration of this freedom. For them, the status quo is a much safer endeavor. They believe that the status quo is a "stable" approach to life. But notice the degree to which they have become stagnant. Is that the life you want?

Once you begin living the miracle you'll want to share it. A word of caution: "preaching" your new way of living is not always appreciated or even effective. It is best to act as a model leader while compassionately approaching those people who are resistant to change. Who you are *being* teaches more than anything you can say.

The more of a leader you are the more you'll notice non-leaders all around you. Give them the space to grow at their own speed. Use this opportunity for compassion. Compassion brings peace to any difference, and as a miracle leader your compassion will be one of your best-used tools. Rather than making others wrong for progressing at different rates, you can recognize that you can only be responsible and accountable for living *your* life as a miracle leader.

Unveiling Gifts

Remember to always go back to the basics. Are you someone who people can count on? Can you imagine what your life would be like if you were? Do you always do what you said you are going to do? Living life as a miracle leader begins with this core practice.

This does not mean that you have to live your life perfectly. But with openness and willingness to grow as a miracle leader, you will demonstrate the attributes of leadership over time. The key to your success in living as a miracle leader is to first accept that no matter what your title is, this process of discovery will unveil gifts you previously never knew you had.

Imagine you are a sales person. Because your integrity in your field of sales is in alignment with the highest good for all those concerned, people feel your positive energy when you walk into a room. People may or may not know why they trust you, but they can see that your intentions are good and that you are a person who keeps his word. All things considered equal, would they be more likely to buy something from a person who reeks of manipulation or a person like you who radiates integrity? The answer is obvious. When living life as a miracle leader, these concepts can be applied in a practical manner.

In this chapter new ways of viewing leadership have been revealed from macro to micro perspectives that support your life. Within you is a leader who demonstrates your true Self. Though this journey to authentic leadership will not require more time of you, it will require that you be willing to see the opportunities for change and growth in every single situation you encounter. You don't have to wait for some big thing to show up. The opportunity will be there in everything.

Are you thinking now that you are comfortable in your life? But yet you somehow know that there is more for you? You'll find what's more by asking, again: What do you want for your Self?

Remember that you always have a choice: You can continue living exactly as you have been or, you can trust me when I say that many have gone before you and if they can do this so can you. By taking your leadership to a new level, phenomenal results will be revealed. You'll discover a new way of being that will engage and inspire the people you care about in a very positive way.

> *" 'Miracles have ceased.' Have they indeed? When? They had not ceased this afternoon when I walked into the wood and got into bright, miraculous sunshine, in shelter from the roaring wind."*
>
> **Ralph Waldo Emerson**

Chapter Nine

Implementing Miracles

What do Batman, Spiderman, Superman, and Wonder Woman all have in common? If you guessed that they are all superheroes, you are correct. If you guessed that they are all action-oriented, you are even more accurate. That is the reason those heroes call to us.

When I was a child, I would dream for hours about what it would be like to have such superpowers. As I grew older, I no longer daydreamed about soaring through the sky. But I still wondered whether or not I embodied unrevealed powers.

Each one of us has the inner yearning to be a person of action, which means we all have the hidden capacity to be a miracle leader. Once we have that understanding, we begin to see the possibilities for living a heroic life.

When I think of heroes in our modern age, I think of miracle leaders like Mother Theresa, Nelson Mandela, Mahatma Gandhi, Albert Einstein, Buckminster Fuller, and Princess Diana as well as many others. Regardless of whether or not I agree with *everything* about their lives, I am fascinated by the clarity with which they took action.

Each of these individuals fulfilled their life's visions by caring about something bigger than themselves. Their dedication to their life dreams impacted millions of people all over the world. They each had the courage to be authentic while standing alone against those who opposed them.

Being a miracle leader is not a popularity contest. It's a demonstration of genuine beliefs.

A True Miracle Leader Story

Recently, I watched a film called *Freedom Writers* about the inner city school teacher Erin Grewell. The teacher is played by Hilary Swank. It's an inspiring true story about a woman who cared so much about her students that she was willing to stand alone while challenging the public school system.

Mrs. Grewell's courageous alternative teaching methods positively changed the lives of her students by disrupting the school district's status quo. For the first time in the students' lives, a teacher had cared enough about them to make a major impact on their hearts and minds. Mrs. Grewell is a modern day miracle leader.

Once you realize that miracle leaders are not just fantasies clad in capes and masks, you will become more and more aware that they are people walking amongst us daily. You will also begin to awaken to the miracle leader inside of your Self, and you will notice that the world is full of people like you who have the courage to make a difference in any given moment.

Life Changing Moments

I am reminded of the famous anonymous quote, "Small things done consistently in strategic places make a major difference." Miracle leaders in our lives do small things over time. But at the end of the day, week, month, year and lifetime, these people will have made major differences. These individuals care so much that they find the courage within to take action when others may not.

In my years of studying leadership I have met many miracle leaders. To me, these are "ordinary people doing extraordinary things." A moment can be transformed by the actions of one person. While this ordinary person may never have been a leader before, they have found their moment to step up and shift the world through their courage.

Taking Action

Miracle leadership is often times most apparent and is in its deepest form when it is most needed—during a crisis. Crisis situations temper and prepare us for greater things. Many leaders of organizations with whom I have worked have gone through periods in their lives when they were "prepared" by crises to better lead in future situations. Each individual demonstrated his courage through action.

Regardless of whether or not you have been confronted with similar situations, you will know when that moment of choice is upon you. How will you decide? What will you do?

I have found that sometimes in these moments of choice I get fearful. I don't want to confront the jerk in the restaurant, or the person dumping his trash in the parking lot. I am afraid that they might punch me in the nose (or light my hair on fire!) I mean these days, who knows? Yet, I find that it is also not worth it to hide somewhere outside of my integrity. While I am of course not recommending that you go into a situation where your safety is in jeopardy, there are daily situations where you could benefit from taking action. Life presents us with many opportunities for courageous acts and miracle leadership. These are the moments I call *choice points*. I know when they have arrived because I usually feel a nervous tension that makes me wish I could ignore the situation rather then acting on it.

Depending upon the nature of the situation, the problem that is presenting me with a choice point won't go away. Though it may not return in the same form, life will test me on this same issue again and again until I have successfully dissolved my fears by taking action.

If you are struggling in your relationship with your boss, it will only prolong the inevitable by avoiding the situation. You need to speak with your boss now. Really. Don't waste another minute. Remember, living your life as a miracle leader requires willingness to become free of the situations that seem to have power over you. By being willing to take action in these situations, you are allowing your Self to be the leader that you naturally are.

Freedom through Choice

Are you at a choice point in your life today? Is there some situation in your life that requires your courage to break through to find freedom on the other side? While there is no secret formula on how to break through, by accessing enough information you will be empowered to address any situation. Then it's time to act. In other words, "punch through it."

While there are several approaches you can take to prepare to meet your choice point, I find the approach that works best for me is when I am focusing myself on being "for" something as opposed to "against" something.

Mother Theresa was a great role model for this approach. Instead of saying that she was "against war," she always exclaimed that she was "for peace." She refused to march in "anti-war" rallies because of that. Though her difference might seem subtle, at this level of leadership it is huge. Because as a leader, it is vital that you offer solutions. Rather than pointing out another's faults, you will find more power in focusing on the areas in which they have succeeded. Then look to transform and build upon the areas of discomfort.

Your solution-finding skills will soon become your way of "being." Your way of being is everything. It's what attracts the life you have. If you focus on problems, you get problems. If you focus on solutions, you get solutions. If you communicate with patience, you get patience.

From cultivating your way of being you will build greater leadership momentum and your actions will get results.

> *"If existence was ever a miracle, then existence is ALWAYS a miracle."*
>
> **Andrew Schwartz**

Chapter Ten

Miracles Through Full Participation

Recently, I attended a workshop in which a person was speaking about not feeling fully utilized in his work. The organization he worked for was not really using him in the right ways.

The facilitator of the workshop did a masterful job of changing the focus of this person from the outside to the inside. He finally got the person to see that he was "just going through the motions" at work. He arrived to work on time, got his pay check, and did what was required of him not to get fired. But he himself was not really "showing up." It wasn't the organization's fault that he felt unfulfilled.

Going through the motions like that is tiring. It steals energy. It does not work long term for the human spirit because we know deep down we are made of pure energy and vitality. We feel unfulfilled whenever we disconnect ourselves from that vitality.

Over the years, I have become a great observer of people. I have also done my own Soul searching. As a result, I have learned that there are basically two ways to live life:

1. Play life safely and avoid making mistakes.
2. Live life "full throttle."

People who live full throttle are participating fully in their lives. They're in love with living, learning and getting to know people. They're not afraid to get hurt because they realize that getting hurt and making mistakes are a part of living a full life. By "letting go" of past constraints, limitations, and resentments, they embrace life.

To participate fully in your own life doesn't mean that you need to be so busy that you overload your schedule. Participating merely means being more "present" and involved in what you choose to do.

For you, this may mean becoming involved in service projects, getting to know your colleagues at work better, or going on a great adventure. Participating fully is an element that each of us can define for ourselves. What will you want to do?

Are You a Lackluster Participant?

Many people I have met want to participate fully in their lives but they are afraid to "put their hearts on the line." They hold themselves back from sharing meaningful ideas. When they check their own feelings, they are either tired, full of fear, or unhappy. They have lost their zest for life, and they no longer participate as leaders. These individuals think they're "saving energy for the right situation," yet their days seem to drag along, and those situations never arrive.

On the other hand there are miracle leaders. They participate fully in every element of their lives. They have enormous amounts of physical and emotional energy, and they wake up looking forward to how they can best contribute to people and situations. They are alive, full of confidence, and filled with joy. These individuals give fully of themselves to each situation, and they are generous with their spirit.

Which group do you identify with? What is your level of participation in life? How involved are you with your family? How much of your personal creativity do you share on work projects? How invested are you in your performance at work? In what positive ways have your personal and professional contributions affected others (i.e. family and work associates)?

Will You Join Me In This Experiment?

The rewards of full participation in life are far-reaching. Miracle leaders can create virtually anything they want. As they begin to influence others through full participation, they experience a sense of "ownership" over results in their lives. They see things more clearly, communicate more freely, and have a strong sense of conviction.

Living life as a miracle leader is not about a *right* way or a *wrong* way rather, it is about finding your way. For example, when I am fully participating in my life, I:

1. Enjoy my work.
2. Love people.
3. Learn something new.
4. Appreciate a beautiful day.
5. Speak my truth.
6. Listen carefully.
7. Take care of my body.
8. Sleep well.
9. Laugh often.
10. Have many friends.

Take a moment to consider your indications of fully participating. What would your list entail?

Now Roll Up Your Sleeves

The principles of miracle leadership involve peeling back layers of beliefs that may or may not serve you as you become present to your own truth.

During this process, there is little room for pretense or posturing. You must be honest with yourself. While you will make mistakes and your life might even get messy, as a miracle leader you will embrace your life in ways that you denied and covered up in the past. During this exhilarating, scary, and revealing process, you will unveil the core truth of your Self. This is a process which no one can do for you. There is incredible value in going through it.

Consulting the Real Expert on "You"

More likely than not, over the years your teachers, parents, friends, and lovers have tried to tell you how you should live your life. They do this because they love you. While they may be trying to help you discover your life's path, only you can know your Self. Nobody knows more about your life than you. Therefore you must learn to trust your Self. Miracle leadership is about gaining access to that part of you that knows—really knows—how *you* want to live.

While at times it may be beneficial to ask others for advice, remember to trust yourself on your own advice. You may feel like having others tell you what to do but if you are constantly looking to others to make your life's decisions, you are no longer fully participating in your own life.

There will also be temptations to tell others what to do. But what is the real value of that? In a word: avoidance. By focusing on them you avoid yourself. It is much easier to disengage yourself from your own situation when you're advising others on theirs. When you do that, you don't have to face your own truths. While projecting your opinions onto others, you lose sight of your own growth opportunities and challenges. By doing this, you are not participating fully as a miracle leader.

Being a Miracle Leader

When miracle leaders participate fully they are continuously learning. Through this learning, they expand their consciousness so that miracles can occur. Continuous learning allows them to expand into the miracle. From this level, they begin to see miracles as a daily occurrence.

Living life as a miracle leader involves a process of acceptance that will bring new power and energy to your life. What if you could accept your Self fully as you are? You could live freely in your thoughts, emotions and experiences. You could stand in your power while simultaneously accepting and supporting others as they express themselves. You could create a life in which you would live fully as you experience miracle after miracle.

With this awareness, you will be more willing to embrace self-exploration as a life-long endeavor. You will feel peace inside of your Self, knowing that you are unique. You can be a miracle leader.

Begin by Taking Off the Brakes

When you are living life as a miracle leader, you are generous with your Self. This involves living with full enthusiasm, even at the risk of appearing more adventurous than the average person. For example, have you ever felt your Self holding back when you felt enthusiastic? When you trust your full participation, you will share your ideas, your creativity, and your leadership.

What if you were to let off of the brakes right now and allow the spirit of your Self be fully expressed? You would tap into your own truth. The part of you that is afraid and holds back is the part that is unnatural, and this is what causes your discomfort.

Now, Now, Now

When thinking about how often people hold back from fulfilling their truth, I am often reminded of the phrase, "If not now, then when?"

The time for you is ***now.***

You are exactly where you should be. The situation is exactly as it should be. *Now* is the time to act. There is no reason to wait, and any "reason" is something you have created out of fear. There is no right time but the present. Share that fantastic idea, speak your truth, and take that step toward your heart's desire.

Are you too old for this? Too young, maybe? It doesn't matter if you are 10 or 110! There is no better time than right now to share your greatest expression of creativity in your job, loving in your relationship, and courage in taking your next step.

> *"It is nothing short of a miracle that modern methods of instruction have not yet entirely strangled the holy curiosity of inquiry."*
>
> **Albert Einstein**

Chapter Eleven

Living in the Spirit of Miracle Leadership

Several months ago I sat on a park bench having a conversation with a woman I had just met. I will call her Sarah. She began speaking to me about what she was witnessing in her life. Until recently, she had thought miracles were just a bunch of b.s. (belief systems).

But while I sat with her, she told me stories from her past that have led her to this place in her life where she needed to make changes. After surrendering to the awareness that there was a different way to live, she began feeling places in her heart open up to the possibility of real transformation.

Sitting with me, a complete stranger, Sarah started to cry. At first she was embarrassed, but as I watched her more closely I witnessed a beautiful change. Sarah's face transformed as she began both releasing her old beliefs about miracles and accepting new possibilities. Years of judgment, negativity, and self blame began to drop away.

After a few moments passed, Sarah looked at me square in the eyes. As her tears welled up, I knew that she had found something inside of herself to which she previously did not have access. By being open to new possibilities in her life, Sarah gave her Self the space to create a miracle.

As I walked away from my conversation with Sarah, I reflected on how steeped in honesty, vulnerability, and integrity our experience was. At that moment, I had a powerful realization that if Sarah could *choose* to create a miracle in her life, then what really is the miracle? Like a cosmic two-by-four, the answer hit me simply and clearly straight between my eyes. The miracle is you. Yes, YOU are the miracle. You are a miracle to be here on this planet. You are the divine leader of your own life, and you can produce changes and create the type of life that you have always wanted. I am a miracle and you are a miracle. Even those individuals who you may think are not miracles are, in fact, miraculous too.

There was a sweet perfection in the simplicity of this realization. We are all miracles of creation who have been given a life to express in whatever way we choose. Because we are each a miracle, we have the ability to create daily miracles. If your life does not feel like a miracle, I recommend that you take an honest look at the choices you have made.

You can have the life that you desire, and the power of change rests inside of you.

By reaffirming your power as a miracle leader, you will change your perception of life and your roles in it. Once you believe that you are truly as unique, powerful and miraculous as your creator intended, you will begin to witness changes in your life. I recommend saying these affirmations out loud. With each statement, "feel" each word you speak.

I am a miracle.
I am a leader of miracles.
I am a miracle to be alive.

While some people may feel uncomfortable with these ideas, I can assure you that there is nothing blasphemous about being a miracle. God has created you to share your goodness with the world. Because God would not have created "garbage," a person is not a "bad" person; rather, they can only behave in a negative manner. Once you believe that you are a miracle, you will begin to see amazing results. In the Bible, God reminds us that we "can do all things" (Philippians 4:13).

Upon reflection of my conversation with Sarah, I realized that I overlook many miracles in my daily life. I recognized that our time on the bench spent speaking about life was a miracle in itself. For Sarah, sharing a conversation with such depth and meaning was a rare occurrence. I told her that I was grateful to have experienced this miracle with her, as I continued to recognize many blessings and miracles in my everyday interactions.

Now I wondered, what would ever stop me from living at this level of realization?

What might intervene and get in the way? And then I saw it: thoughts! It was only a thought that stood between me and living my life as a miracle.

Let me give you an example:

Stories Versus Reality

I recently hired a team of painters to paint my home while I was out of town. Before leaving for my trip, I questioned whether or not I should call the owner of the painting company, as I had not heard yet whether they had agreed to the contract.

I was frustrated with the company because I was in a time crunch. I began to create "stories" in my mind about why the boss had not contacted me, and before too long I had determined that this company was not well organized. Before calling them, my frustration had quickly cycled into deprecating thoughts, which in turn left me feeling anxious and deflated.

Finally, I decided to make the phone call. And to my great surprise and relief, I found out that they had been trying to reach me all along. It was just that the spam filter on my email account had been blocking all their communications!

Now I thought about the life energy and precious time I wasted with all those negative thoughts about that company. I was amazed at what I did to myself for no reason. Experiences like this have caused me to reevaluate my relationship with my thoughts. Maybe thinking doesn't have to be so automatic.

Scientists have proven that human beings, on average, produce 42 thoughts per minute, which is equivalent to 60,000 thoughts per day, 21, 900,000 thoughts per year and 219,000,000 thoughts every ten years. Now, that's a lot of thoughts!

Imagine how much time you spend "thinking" thoughts. Of these thoughts, what percentage of them is berating yourself? What percent are praising? Are you in control over that? Or do your thoughts just pop up like bad television commercials?

If you could change anything about your thought process, what would it be?

The Power of Thoughts

Over the years, I have become more and more aware of the power of the mind. When confronted by an uncomfortable situation in the past I would either become anxious and full of fear or I would become angry and defensive. And it was always because of the array of thoughts running through my mind. I automatically responded to my thoughts and emotions as if they were the absolute truth.

I couldn't have been more wrong. Thoughts are just thoughts. And because our minds are such powerful tools and have such amazing abilities to store information as linear constructs, we aren't always aware of how automatically our thought patterns kick in. Once we remember a person, situation, or feeling, our minds reflexively bring up information which we assume is factual.

But is it really factual? When we review all of our daily thoughts, is it practical to believe that everything our mind thinks is true? Not only is it impractical, it can poison our existence with stress and resentment. Because although a thought might "feel" true, it is just a perception of our emotions which we give value to as the ultimate truth.

To get out of this thinking trap, I challenge you to do three things: 1. Act as a witness of your emotions, and watch your thoughts as though you were watching a movie, 2. Look within for your inner truth because your ego thrives from telling your mind false stories about your Self and others, and 3. Ask your Self if your thoughts are kind and loving.

If you find your thoughts are judgmental or negative, understand that this is not representative of your true being. Instead, turn your focus to love and trust the power of your spiritual inward leader.

The Power of Prayer

During my Spiritual Psychology Master's Program at the University of Santa Monica, my friend and professor Dr. Ron Hulnick would often say, "If you are going to have a fantasy about something, make sure you win at it."

In other words, emotions are malleable and they are *our own creations.*

If my mind is wandering and has questionable thoughts, how can I, as a responsible leader, get true information? What can I trust as guidance for my decisions?

As leaders, we can base our decisions on many factors. For example, we will most likely have knowledge from past experiences, prior researched information, and suggestions from our colleagues. While these are all valuable resources, sometimes they won't be enough. What then? What do you do when all physical level approaches seem limiting?

I would like you to consider a more inward approach of prayer.

The most powerful source of information that I have available to me is through my relationship with Spirit. I am able to access my miracle leader by being open to my belief in a divine power.

Universal Beliefs

Patricia Aburdene's influential book *Megatrends 2010* demonstrates the necessity for individual spiritual growth in one's professional career. In her chapter titled "The Power of Spirituality-From Personal to Organizational," Aburdene writes, "Millions have invited Spirit into their lives, through personal growth, religion, meditation, prayer, or yoga. The result is a values shift that is measurable and monumental. A 2004 Gallup survey found that 90 percent of Americans believe in God; it jumps to 95 percent when people are asked, 'or a universal Spirit.'"

If 9 out of 10 Americans believe in something "universal," the possibilities for Spirit's work in miracle leadership are profound. Imagine the exciting new levels of team leadership when collaboration is synonymous with divine inspiration.

While it is sometimes difficult to stay focused on the miracles of this world, by centering my thoughts on God, Spirit, Lord, or the Universe, I am always returned to the joy of my life's purpose. Though I want to live my life fully aware of global affairs, I also want to envelop my Self in positive surroundings so that I may make constructive contributions.

Living life as a miracle leader allows me to see the benefits in every situation. Through this way of living, positive outcomes are *created* and leave me feeling a sense of something magical. These magical feelings can be achieved on a daily basis through the work of Spirit.

Being Compassionate and Forgiving

I also have become aware that I will make mistakes on this journey. Like most people, I will judge myself for making these mistakes. But when I am willing to use every situation to my ultimate benefit, I find that I can both easily forgive myself as well as move to the next area of my life.

Because I have a relationship with Spirit, I am provided with consistent motivation as well as a larger perspective on areas in my life where I transgress. I can always forgive myself for and learn from my mistakes, move into greater acceptance, and continue my life's purpose.

Almost three years ago, I went through a divorce. It was a hard time in my life. I was confused, scared, and I judged myself because I had never thought I would be a man who divorced his wife. At times I questioned my core being whether I was in or out of my integrity to progress with my divorce. While our societal standards would suggest that getting a divorce is not the "right" thing to do, I have learned a great deal about being in and valuing my own personal integrity over and above the standards of society.

This process deepened my compassion as I learned to forgive myself and others for all judgments. I have heard my friend John-Roger say, "Forgiveness is the key to the Kingdom." By living in a space of forgiveness, I become free from my self-defeating hell. Had it not been for my relationship with God, I would have had a difficult time maintaining any semblance of balance during this time in my life.

I continue to be amazed by the power of having a foundational spiritual practice. Once I allow Spirit to work in my life, profound things occur. For example, I recently had dinner with my girlfriend, my new friend and her new boyfriend. My new friend is my former wife, Sally.

Had I remained in a place of self-deprecation, I quite possibly would not have been sharing laughter around that dinner table. Instead, I grow tremendously from these experiences, and I continue to seek the perfection of every situation. By living life as a miracle leader, my strong beliefs in the divine free me of my suffering.

To grow both as a person and leader, it is my experience that a spiritual practice is vital to one's development. Whether you meditate, pray, read the Bible or other inspiring books, take long walks in nature, or write in a journal, it is important that you find the areas in your life that bring you the most peace. To sustain a strong connection with God, I recommend that you consistently do at least one spiritual practice. For example, I vigilantly read one prayer every day. As I recite the prayer out loud, I can usually feel my heart opening to the essence of who I am as man and as a leader. My heart area begins to warm, and I feel my heart swelling with love.

For You

I have written an ecumenical prayer, which can be applied to various spiritual beliefs. If you choose to use this prayer or to commit to your own prayer, notice the difference it makes. Notice the difference it makes in you after you initially read it. Then notice how changes are beginning to occur in your life when you begin your day with this prayer:

****

Leadership Prayer

Dear Spirit,

Give me the courage to lead my Self on this day. It is my intention to be of service to others through my leadership. I ask for the strength to love in all situations as well as to be compassionate with my own process of growth. Give me the heart to be honest with people in each moment, while staying true to my own integrity. Help me bring leadership to all situations, and support me in listening to the truth that resonates deep in my heart. I ask that you bless me with grace and guide me in being the man/woman you would have me be. Illumine for me my transgressions, and give me the strength and power to make the necessary changes.Give me focus on what is most meaningful, and support me in smiling upon my own adversity while guiding me to understand peacefully all challenges. I pray to forgive myself and others for any and all past mistakes, and I ask to begin this moment with an experience of miraculous leadership.

God, I pray for your grace as I contribute to my business, my family, my community and/or my life. Thank you, Spirit, for the blessings that are bestowed upon me as I become more confident in living my life as a leader. I pray all of this always and only for the highest good of all concerned.

****

Making the Unbelievable Believable

Open your mind and experiment with reading this prayer for thirty days. What do you have to lose? Here's what you have to gain: you will begin to see noticeable changes and results. Prayer will support how you experience your life.

For me, it has increased the tangible results in my business and life. If you are already practicing prayer, perhaps this will validate what you already know; you can take prayer to a new level by committing to increased levels either in different areas of your life or by praying more often throughout the day. If you do not practice prayer regularly, you have nothing to lose and everything to gain by committing a mere two minutes per day. Do you know of anything else that is this simple and will improve your standard of joy? Believe in the unbelievable, and know that you have the power to create these possibilities in your life.

Roger Banister is one great example of a man who challenged the "impossible" by being the first person to run a mile in under four minutes. Before breaking the mile record, Roger spoke with doctors and scientists about the human physiology in order to determine the possibility of fulfilling his dream. While many specialists told him he could not do it because it was physically impossible, Banister did not believe the evidence, and instead he set out a process by which he trained his body, mind and spirit to accomplish what was believed by others to be beyond unreasonable.

After Roger Banister broke the world record in the mile run, his leadership in the running world "opened the door" for other runners to challenge the *impossible.* What is so fascinating is that once it became deemed possible to break the four-minute mile, several world-class runners also did so shortly after Roger's accomplishment.

To understand this example, I would like to encourage you to consider the difference between the following statements:

Seeing is Believing
Believing is Seeing

A classic management truism, *Seeing is Believing* can be defined as needing to first witness something before knowing it's true. See how often you approach situations from this habitual perspective. An example of this might be, "Prove that you are a championship team, and then I will build the stadium."

While there is nothing right or wrong about this approach, I would like you to consider the outcome of this type of approach. How would this situation have differed had you approached it by first believing then seeing? ("I believe in this team, so we are building a stadium.") Would your relationships with yourself and others shift?

A majority of our society bases its choices and decisions on this kind of "prove it to me first" mindset. Do you think we are limiting our possibilities with this approach? How can you take this understanding of our society to empower your own leadership?

Believing is Seeing

Individuals who create, maintain, and share their visions with others are miracle leaders. They are the Roger Banisters of the world who have the courage and inner drive to say "No" to limitations and "Yes" to possibilities. He believed he could break the barrier then he saw that he could. Not the other way around!

By first believing in the power of possibility, leaders like Bannister manifest their dreams through belief, intention, focus, method, application and *then* result. To be a successful leader who achieves the "impossible," practice the following actions:

1. Believe in something with full conviction.

2. Intend a positive outcome.

3. Focus on your aspiration.

4. Determine how you will accomplish it.

5. Take consistent actions.
6. Enjoy your results.

Believing is Seeing will also involve engaging others in your beliefs. But soon you'll develop a track record for *results* which will allow others to both see and achieve.

Can you think of any great business leaders who at first were considered radical for their visionary ideas? What would it take for you to be one of these rare visionaries? Would you feel comfortable with this type of business approach? Your vision may range anywhere from creating a new and innovative product to shifting the mindset of believability in individuals through your actions as a leader.

Your Vision

As you deepen your ability to produce results through your vision, you will ultimately begin to see the common thread in how to *create an outcome* based on your beliefs. While your methods or strategies may differ with each case, you can maintain an underlying principle that whatever you believe in can be created. You will begin to experience a feeling of possibility inside of your Self that is integrated with your intellectual knowledge.

Listen to your ideas with respect. Don't squelch them with previous thoughts of what is not achievable.I'm sure you have witnessed hundreds of situations where someone's idea is quickly opposed. That's the norm. But as a miracle leader you will be learning to trust your own intuition. You'll learn to trust that the spirit of your idea is worthy of discussion. While initially you may have few supporters, you can get good at finding ways to engage others in the possibility of what you believe in. Your idea doesn't even need to be fully developed. Just believe and you'll soon see where it leads. As you practice this process, you will cultivate a very deep trust in your Self.

You are the Miracle

Have you ever prayed to God for a miracle, or wished that things could just change for you? Have you ever wished that you could just get rid of all of your personal and professional problems? How would your life be different if your wish miraculously came true?

To produce a miracle, first be open to the idea that miracles do happen in modern day life. Look to see miracles, and the more you look the more evidence you will find that will keep you believing. By first believing, you will have the confirmation of seeing which will keep you believing.

But how do you first move toward experiencing a miracle? The answer is simple: Be present. Be awake. Be aware in your daily life. Reflect upon your interactions with curiosity while recognizing the many blessings that occur.

> *"Miracles happen to those who believe in them."*
>
> **Bernard Berenson**

Chapter Twelve

Loving is the Miracle

Recently my good friend and teacher John Morton told me an inspiring story. Waiting in a long line at the grocery store, a young child begged his mother to buy various things which she did not want to buy for him. As the child continued to persist, the mother began to lose her temper. Her temper quickly developed into anger and border-line rage. While the people in line witnessed this situation, no one knew what to do.

The mother was so angry that it seemed as though she was going to hit the child. Her anger was escalating. While the people in line stood in awe not knowing what their responsibilities were, something magical occurred. A man stepped out of the line, and in a voice that commanded presence he yelled at the top of his lungs, **"Kindness!"** The mother was stunned. The store grew silent. The situation was no more.

This man had performed an act of love and leadership. He made his point dramatically without even physically intervening. The mother quickly came to her senses with this one simple word. Was that a small miracle? You decide.

For many years, I have led public seminars on leadership all over the country. I have met thousands of people in a variety of industries. In these sessions, they reveal that in their personal lives they are parents, siblings, friends, spouses, etc. But they see their personal lives as separate from their professional lives. In other words, they are different people at work than they are at home.

As a typical seminar progressed, someone inevitably discovers that leadership is not something that happens only at work. Leadership occurs everywhere. It's an organic life process.

Many people have found that these principles of leadership aren't restricted to managing the office. They can implement these same values at home. Leadership can be applied to all parts of life.

As a miracle leader, you will feel a fire emblazoned within by your human spirit. Your love for integrity, truth, and the process of learning will continue growing daily. While leadership is not always easy, and it most certainly is not the romantic vision of the charismatic individual from a Hollywood film, you will find the strength within your Self to make incredible contributions at work, at home, and in your community.

By loving who you are and what you do, you will be contributing a shared energy that can make miracles happen. But if you don't love who you are, you can't lead from love nor can you be a positive and effective leader.

Trusting Love

If you want to lead your life, your business, and your family, you must embrace each area of life with all of your heart and soul. You must be open to the full process of learning which includes receiving constructive feedback from people and allowing yourself to be vulnerable. You will naturally become more vulnerable as you begin to express your truest freedom. You'll learn to actually look forward to coming "face-to-face" with your greatest fears.

When fears are present you are usually afraid of change. So recognize when they are present. Ask your Self, "By having this fear, what am I missing out on? If I did not have this fear, how would my life be different?" From there, you can become aware of your fear "triggers" so that you can instead focus on love. I have often heard that fear is one of the most powerful things in our world, but even fear is afraid of love.

Love stands tall beside the ever-ready fear, even though we too often fall victim to fear (because we forget love's power.) We overlook love because fear is at the forefront of our minds. It surrounds us in our everyday lives. It disguises itself by taking on forms such as anger, depression, hatred, jealousy, and greed. Because we are so accustomed to living in fear, love is often viewed as being "touchy-feely." And by minimizing love that way, we miss its power and strength.

No More "Mr. Tough Guy"

I would like to challenge this typical "touchy-feely" perception of love. We have falsely labeled love as an emotion or a feeling. I would like you to consider love in a new way: love is a *behavior* that is *productive.*

That's right. Love is productive. If you want to be a more productive and inspiring person, your most effective behavioral choice would be to love.

If you have believed otherwise, give it a test. If you have believed that the most effective behavioral choice for you is intimidation through anger, try this new way. Maybe you've already noticed that people are not responding to your intimidation and anger, because, quite simply, they don't have to. They can easily pick up their lives and move on, only leaving you with more responsibilities than one person could ever handle. So stop it. Stop the "tough guy" act and open your heart to a new way of being. Everyone in your life will thank you.

Big LOVE, Little fear

I have been in many situations where I was afraid to say or do anything. Yet, when I chose to believe strongly in something, I would overcome those fears and act as an effective and courageous leader. My *love* for what I feel is right would become more important than my own fear.

My study of love and miracle leadership has taught me several valuable things:

1. Fear and love have differing energies that get very different results.
2. When I have chosen to live from a place of trust and respect, I embody the same energy as love.
3. Not only did the man who yelled "kindness" change the lives of the mother and little boy, but he also made a difference in the lives of those waiting in line as well as anyone who has been told this story.
4. Our world is ready for more acts of love.

Loving Your Life

When you live from your heart, you will find that you will love your life. You will love leadership. You will find that you are creating a life of miracles. For, as Dr. Martin Luther King, Jr. eloquently said:

Everyone can be great because anyone can serve. You don't have to have a college degree to serve. You don't even have to make your subject and verb agree to serve....You only need a heart full of grace, a soul generated by love.

As your leader within begins to unfold, you will bear witness to miraculous events taking place in your daily life. You will lose fear of life, and you will live from an incredible place of love, compassion, and kindness.

Therefore I now ask you, what do you love? What do you believe in with solid conviction? What would make you stand in a grocery store and yell the word "kindness" at the top of your lungs to make a major impact? Miracle leadership requires loving something with all of your heart.

After studying leaders for the past 17 years, I have learned without exception that everyone loves what they believe in. Teachers, CEO's, professional athletes, and spiritual figures, for example, are all driven by the behavior of love. Find out what you love. And if you have trouble finding it, slow down and remember what it was like to be a child. Love from that place of innocence, and know that with each act of love, you are choosing a new way of being.

The Perfection of Love

You are perfect just as you are. The perfection of the Self is ever present. As a miracle leader, you will get in touch with your Self through love. In the book, *When Are You Coming Home? A Personal Guide to Soul Transcendence*, John-Roger and Pauli Sanderson write:

I created my path to freedom. I saw that the Soul was masterful at accepting and experiencing whatever was presented. I saw that the Soul exemplifies purest loving because it does not judge any choice and recognizes that there is learning with every choice (117-118).

Love is a choice. So be aware when you are faced with "choice points" between fear and love. It can happen at anytime: in a meeting, on the phone, or when you are driving. Being a miracle leader does not mean that you won't experience fear; but it does mean you will learn more readily to choose love. By choosing love, you will experience greater levels of peace and calmness inside of your Self. As a miracle leader, your love will inspire other people into positive actions.

Being loving does not make you a wimp; instead, it makes you strong and full of conviction. As a miracle leader, performing acts of love may include telling the compassionate truth to a colleague. Through this, you are challenging the status quo by addressing cynical office behavior.

More and more evidence proves that there is a strong link between love and results. The most respectful and functional teams I've worked with embody this quality of love for their work. This is not just a theory. It's an application: by loving as a miracle leader, you will be more effective, more productive, and your results will be greater.

Thank You

It has been a joy for me to write this book. I have loved being a part of your life as you have gone through this process with me. And now it's time for you to take ownership of the miracle leader that you are. You will enjoy the great humility and compassion that accompany the twelve elements of miracle leadership. You will soon realize that you do have the ability to be a miracle leader if you are willing.

I want to thank you personally for completing this book and for having the courage to see the best in your Self and in others. I wish you the best on your journey of miracle leadership, and I look forward to learning about your many successes. Miracles abound!

With love and respect,

Stephen P. McGhee

> *"Where there is great love there are always miracles."*
>
> **Willa Cather**

EXERCISES

The following exercises are designed to deepen your experience of this book. I invite you to answer these questions with complete honesty and integrity as you continue your journey of Living Life as a Miracle Leader.

If you become true to your Self and your path of life leadership, you will begin to notice great changes and miracles in your life. Your attachments will fall away, and you will make room for new experiences.

Exercise Number One:

1. What area in my life must I let go to grow more fully into my "Life Leadership"?
2. What one thing would I be willing to let go of this week?
3. What positive benefits might I foresee?
4. During the next week, I will keep track of my experience as I let go of something to which I am attached.

Exercise Number Two:

Take a few moments to answer the following questions about your life:

1. In what areas of your life could you challenge your comfort level?
2. What possibilities could you create if you lived more outside of your comfort level?
3. Write a paragraph on what it would be like to "live into" a vision of being unreasonable. In other words, write about your vision as though it has already occurred. How would you live your life differently if you were outside of your comfort zone?

Now take a minute to reread your paragraph, and sit with the new possibilities for your life. Give your Self the life that you have always wanted. I know this can happen because I live a life that I dreamed possible.

Exercise Number Three:

1. On a scale of 1 to 100 (with 100 being "fully" on course), what is the level of integrity you are currently experiencing in your daily life?
2. In what areas in your life are you "off course" with your integrity?
3. What would you need to do, say, or complete to be "on course"?
4. Specifically, when will you be willing to take this next step to get "on course" with your integrity?
5. What gives you that spark in your life? List at least three things you either do or could do to increase the level of integrity in your life?
6. Are you willing to do any of them? If so, when?

Exercise Number Four:

1. Read the following scenario.

   Consider that many things in life are created through ideas. Ideas then turn to thoughts, thoughts turn to a conversation, and a conversation turns into a meeting of people to develop an idea. There is essentially a full circle that occurs for an idea or thought to be executed as a reality in the area of communication. The only way to ensure that the entire circle of communication is complete and efficient is if the circle is made up of two or more people *who keep their word.*

Contemplate how this practically relates to your life or business.

2. How can you ensure that more of your ideas move from generation to execution?

3. How would your business or home life function differently if you kept your word?

Words are powerful. I am my word, and you are your word. Consider spending an hour today letting your family, friends, and colleagues know how much you appreciate them. Be open to the miracles that bloom after you plant the seed of your word.

Exercise Number Five:

1. What specific method supports you in maintaining a quiet mind?

2. How often do you need to do this practice to stay present with your Self?

3. What is the value of bringing presence to your listening?

4. What is your level of commitment to becoming a great listener?

Exercise Number Six:

1. Take a moment to determine an area of your life in which you want to improve (finances, spirituality, relationship, wellness, job, or adventure).

2. Once you have determined a specific area of focus, find a specific situation within this area in which you want to improve. (For example, you may want to improve your wellness by focusing on what you eat.)

3. Next, answer the following question: "What do I want in the area of wellness?" (You may answer, "I want to go to the Optimal Health Institute for three weeks this year to learn more about the specific benefits of a balanced diet.")

4. Finally, ask yourself the next question: "What am I willing to do to go to the Optimal Health Institute for three weeks this year?" (You may answer, "I am willing to: 1. schedule, participate and pay for my transportation, lodging, and wellness education, and 2. take the necessary time off from work to learn about food and heal my body at the institute.)

These questions can be practiced on a continual basis. They can become a part of your daily routine. Soon you will find—with this daily practice—your objectives will become more attainable as you grow more aligned in your integrity. As you begin to lead from a place of willingness, you will find clarity in all areas of your life. Remember that miracles come from clarity...and clarity comes from Self.

Exercise Number Seven:

To gain the full benefits of these attributes, answer the following questions as they apply practically to your life.

1. How do you define miracle leadership?

2. Without "cheating," can you list at least five elements of a miracle leader?

3. Do you embody different degrees of each of these?

4. What value would there be in your life if you demonstrated the elements of miracle leadership?

5. What are three practical steps you can take today to engage your miracle leadership through these elements?

   For example,

   a. Share your enthusiasm about a situation that others are cynical about.

   b. Point out three solutions to a problem where your co-workers can only see the problem.

   c. Have a revealing and honest conversation with a friend that you have been avoiding. Be compassionate.

6. Take a few minutes to reflect on how these three practical steps will influence your professional and/or personal relationships.

Exercise Number Eight:

In reflection, please take a few minutes to answer the following questions.

1. Are you willing to commit yourself to a solution-based approach when working through areas of conflict?
2. As a miracle leader, what do you stand for?
3. Once you have defined what you stand for in your life, I challenge you to take an action toward that conviction. For example, if you stand for love then go out in the world and act lovingly toward someone who is struggling with being kind to you. Notice how you feel when you are courageous in the face of adversity.

Exercise Number Nine:

1. In the past, what events have you participated in with all of your heart, body, mind and spirit? Briefly describe the experiences you had. What were the tangible results of these experiences? (i.e. Did you win the game? Did you finish the project on time?)

2. In the past, what events have you participated in with only a part of your heart, body, mind and spirit? Briefly describe the experiences you had. What were the tangible results of these experiences? (i.e. Did you win the game? Did you finish the project on time?)

3. In what areas of your life would you like to participate more fully? How will you know when are fully participating? What will be different? What might you expect the outcomes to be?

Exercise Number Ten:

1. How do you define a miracle?
2. Have you created a miracle in your life?
3. If so, what was your experience of creating a miracle?
4. How did you manifest this occurrence?
5. How would you produce a miracle again?
6. If you haven't experienced one personally, have you witnessed a miracle in the lives of others?
7. In what specific area of your life would you like to create a miracle?

Throughout the next week, I encourage you to both repeat your affirmations and become present to the possibility of miracles occurring in your life. By *Believing then Seeing,* you are steps closer to your greatest desires and ideal life.

About The Author

Stephen McGhee has devoted his life to the business of transformation. He has studied the threads to success in many diverse businesses and has spent the last fifteen years guiding executives and their teams to positive, measurable results.With over 10 years of business background on the executive level, Stephen offers a grounded blend of both reality and possibility. His Leadership Coaching is based in reality, not theory.

Stephen has a degree in finance and a Masters degree in Psychology. The qualities that he brings to the table include genuine compassion, sharp intelligence, an engaging presentation style, rock solid integrity, honest and open communication, and his unwavering commitment to living a life of outstanding leadership.

Stephen lives in the Denver area and is available for private individual or executive team coaching as well as keynote speeches.

More about Stephen McGhee Leadership

Conventional approaches - to anything - do not produce the most profound and effective results. True leadership produces meaningful outcomes that are magnificently beyond what most people think are possible. These are the results that stop people in their tracks and inspire a hushed "wow"! Stephen McGhee Leadership is about supporting you into that kind of leadership.

If this doesn't sound like the usual approach of an ex-corporate senior executive with a degree in finance and years of success coaching top leaders - you're right. It's not. If you are looking for usual, then you are not looking for us.

Exactly what do we do?

If we are a fit, we will coach your life or business into an unreasonable vision of excellence that is supported by pragmatic strategies using breakthrough objectives and soul-filled communication for dramatic and radical results.

We work with people who are not satisfied with "better"; they are committed to accomplishing revolutionary results personally and organizationally. We work with leaders who are ready to break through to a whole new way of "being".

Interested in a shift to unreasonably effective leadership?

Check us out on the web at www.mcgheeleadership.com

Email Stephen at Stephen@mcgheeleadership.com

Or give us a call at 303-893-1773.

We look forward to transforming your life!

Here's what a few of Stephen's clients have said:

"My year working with Stephen proved to be one of the most transformative and productive of my life. Stephen's practical, insightful and spiritual approach to personal growth lead me to see beyond the limits of my own self imposed boundaries. That transformation lead to increased financial prosperity, more rewarding personal and professional relationships, and an overall acceptance and appreciation for my own unique company." **–Dave Zobl, VP Sales, NRC Broadcasting**

"Stephen McGhee has worked with our company for many years. Without fail, every seminar has inspired our team and pushed our company to a new level. The difference between Steve and other consultants is his keen ability to involve our team in realistic discussions regarding personal and business growth. The real success in his work occurs away from our session, back in our daily lives as the insight he gives us is practical, useful and meaningful." **–David Strumminger, President / CEO, Mohenis Services**

"Working with Stephen allowed me to move from general management to true leadership. Stephen understood, well before I did, that I needed to "get out of the box" and focus on high-level strategy and results, instead of the day-to-day tasks and accomplishments. I'm grateful that he used a more empathetic, personal approach that helped me see beyond management mechanics and to view myself through a different lens. Stephen has not only helped me grow my own career, but has helped me grow the careers of those that I work with.**–Rick Holzli, General Manager, Microsoft**

Printed in the United States
106004LV00003B/235/P

9 781434 36641